DATE DUE

Making Public Places Safer

Making Public Places Safer

Surveillance and Crime Prevention

Brandon C. Welsh

David P. Farrington

OXFORD
UNIVERSITY PRESS

2009

OXFORD
UNIVERSITY PRESS

Oxford University Press, Inc., publishes works that further
Oxford University's objective of excellence
in research, scholarship, and education.

Oxford   New York
Auckland   Cape Town   Dar es Salaam   Hong Kong   Karachi
Kuala Lumpur   Madrid   Melbourne   Mexico City   Nairobi
New Delhi   Shanghai   Taipei   Toronto

With offices in
Argentina   Austria   Brazil   Chile   Czech Republic   France   Greece
Guatemala   Hungary   Italy   Japan   Poland   Portugal   Singapore
South Korea   Switzerland   Thailand   Turkey   Ukraine   Vietnam

Published by Oxford University Press, Inc.
198 Madison Avenue, New York, New York 10016

www.oup.com

Oxford is a registered trademark of Oxford University Press

Library of Congress Cataloging-in-Publication Data
Welsh, Brandon, 1969–
Making public places safer : surveillance and crime prevention /
Brandon C. Welsh, David P. Farrington.
    p.   cm.—(Studies in crime and public policy)
Includes bibliographical references and index.
ISBN 978-0-19-532621-5
1. Crime prevention—United States.   2. Public spaces—
United States.   3. Public safety—United States.
4. Security systems.   5. Closed circuit television.
I. Farrington, David P.   II. Title.
HV7431.W398 2009
364.4—dc22   2009002630

9 8 7 6 5 4 3 2 1

Printed in the United States of America
on acid-free paper

Acknowledgments

This book is a product of our long-standing concern that the highest quality scientific research available should be put at center stage in political and policy decisions about preventing crime. It is also a product of our ongoing program of research on surveillance for crime prevention in public space. We hope that the marriage of these increasingly important and topical issues will advance knowledge and encourage more effective and just public policy.

Funding support in the form of grants from Sweden's National Council for Crime Prevention (NCCP) and a private foundation were instrumental in the completion of the research for this book. We are particularly grateful to Jan Andersson, director-general of the NCCP, and Mark Steinmeyer.

Along the way, we received sage advice and insightful comments from a number of colleagues, including Anthony Braga, Ron Clarke, Paul Ekblom, Martin Gill, Peter Grabosky, Ross Homel, Jerry Lee, Mark Lipsey, Lawrence Sherman, Chris Sullivan, David Weisburd, and David Wilson. We also benefited from excellent research assistance from Mark Mudge, Katherine Harrington, and Sean O'Dell, and first-class secretarial support from Maureen Brown and Joanne Garner.

Finally, a special debt of gratitude is owed to Michael Tonry as well as James Cook, our brilliant editor at Oxford University Press, who helped us refine our thoughts early on and provided valuable guidance as the writing came to a close.

Contents

Making Public Places Safer

Introduction

1

By the time they were arrested on October 24, 2002, John Allen Muhammad, 41, and his teenage accomplice, Lee Boyd Malvo, had shot and killed 10 people and critically injured another 3 in the Washington, D.C., metropolitan area. Dubbed by the media as the D.C.-area sniper (just one individual was thought to be involved), the perpetrators used a modified car as a sniper's nest and shot victims indiscriminately, including a 13-year-old boy who had just been dropped off at his school, a bus driver taking a break from his route, a man cutting the grass at a car dealership, and a woman returning to her vehicle after shopping at a home building store. The shootings lasted a little more than three weeks, terrorizing residents and captivating the nation. Because it was only a year after the September 11, 2001, terrorist attacks, speculation quickly grew that the snipers were part of a terrorist cell.

Federal, state, and local police forces from across the D.C. area were mobilized, checkpoints were established, sometimes bringing traffic to a standstill for miles, and hundreds of tips were followed up. Criminal profilers were consulted, and a wealth of information was communicated to the public to advise them to be vigilant and to ask for their assistance in the investigation.

With several people already dead and the country's capital region becoming increasingly fearful, police turned to closed-circuit television (CCTV) surveillance cameras in an effort to help them identify and apprehend the suspects. The police reviewed hundreds of hours of footage from cameras at stores, banks, buildings, and traffic cameras at intersections near the shooting sites, as well as from cameras in police cruisers that responded to the shootings. Additionally, CCTV cameras at gas stations and other businesses, once used to protect these private premises from theft and other minor crimes, were being pointed toward parking lots and public streets to deter shots from being fired at their customers and to capture the snipers on tape. The police even enlisted the assistance of the U.S. military. Two army aircraft with the latest surveillance capabilities were used in the search for the vehicle that the police believed the snipers were using (Wolfe, 2002).

Although CCTV cameras did not play a direct role in the eventual arrest of the snipers, this method of public area surveillance was showcased to the American public and police authorities across the country more than in any other high-profile crime. CCTV was fast becoming an important (and accepted) method to make public places safer from crime. In reporting on the D.C.-area sniper case, journalist Elizabeth Wolfe (2002) had this to say: "Whether human eyes or cameras eventually provide a break in this case, one thing remains certain: Surveillance in public places is becoming more prevalent as the technology improves and becomes more affordable."

Five years later, CCTV cameras were used in an effort to help address an altogether different but equally tragic episode of criminal violence in public places. In the midst of what some described as an epidemic of violence that left 26 Chicago public schoolchildren dead (23 by gunfire) and many more injured during the 2007/2008 school year, the city's mayor, police department, and Board of Education embarked on an ambitious plan to connect the more than 4,500 cameras in public schools to police headquarters, the city's 911 emergency center, and police squad cars (*Converge Magazine*, 2008). The program, funded by the federal Department of Homeland Security, allows police to monitor cameras on the outside of buildings around the clock; cameras inside the school can only be viewed in the event of an emergency.

For the 200 or so Chicago public schools that are connected to cameras, which includes all the high schools and some elementary schools and administrative buildings, this represents an important advance. In particular, the cameras had not previously been monitored; tapes could only be viewed *after* an incident. Also, the cameras previously could only be monitored at the Board of Education's central office. The initiative called for more security personnel to be hired and placed in the most difficult schools. The Chicago public school system employs about 1,800 full-time security personnel. An additional 153 Chicago police officers are deployed at 75 schools (Associated Press, 2008).

These two examples of the use of CCTV surveillance, among many others that are taking place across the country, are redefining how public places are being altered to make them safer from crime. In the last few years, the United States has experienced nothing short of an explosive growth in the use of CCTV systems in a wide range of public places, including city and town centers, public transportation systems, public housing communities, parks, and schools (Ratcliffe, 2006; Savage, 2007). This has been met with high levels of public support. An ABC News and *Washington Post* national poll conducted in July 2007 found that 7 out of every 10 (71%) Americans support increased use of surveillance cameras in public places to reduce crime; only 25% of respondents opposed it (*Washington Post*, 2007).

This is a relatively new development in the United States. It was only a few years back that scholars and journalists were writing about how Americans were less accepting and more apprehensive of "Big Brother" implications arising from this surveillance technology (Murphy, 2002; Rosen, 2004). In the United Kingdom, however, there has been long-standing, high-level of support for the use of CCTV cameras in public settings to prevent crime (Gill and Spriggs, 2005; Norris and Armstrong, 1999; Phillips, 1999). The James Bulger case, where two older boys abducted a three-year-old, contributed to this. A recent *Chicago Tribune* editorial perhaps best captures American's changing view toward public area CCTV surveillance:

> We're not sure which is more remarkable, that rapid expansion
> of surveillance, or the public's acceptance of it. Citizens
> occasionally complain to the city that a camera is unsightly—
> but never that it's intrusive. To the contrary, Chicagoans have
> become so demanding that, if a camera comes out of service
> for repair, Ruiz's [head of Chicago's Office of Emergency

Management and Communications] staffers try to replace it with a spare, a loaner. If they don't, he says, the neighbors (and their alderman) are on the phone: "We want our camera back." Whether because of comfort or complacency, some Chicagoans' early fears of Orwellian spying evidently have dwindled. (*Chicago Tribune*, 2008)

Effectiveness and Social Costs

Amid the growing use and support for public area CCTV in the United States and other Western countries, questions have been raised about its effectiveness in preventing crime. This is a particularly contentious issue in the United Kingdom, where public spending on CCTV has far surpassed £250 million (approximately $375 million at the time of this writing) in the past decade. Less is known about public expenditure on CCTV in the United States, but recent figures from major cities suggest that the annual cost could be far in excess of $100 million. Moreover, in the United Kingdom there has long been concern that funding for CCTV has been based partly on a handful of apparently successful schemes that were usually evaluated with weak designs, conducted with varying degrees of competence (Armitage, Smyth, and Pease, 1999) and varying degrees of professional independence from government (Ditton and Short, 1999).

This state of affairs relates directly to one of the chief aims of this book: To argue the case that the highest quality scientific research available should be center stage in political and policy decisions about funding and implementing CCTV (and other crime prevention surveillance measures) in an effort to make public places safer from crime. This is very much about contributing to evidence-led policy, and it has ramifications beyond the immediate subject matter covered here. We believe that crime prevention should be rational and based on the best possible evidence. An evidence-based approach involves using the highest quality evaluation research and the most rigorous scientific methods to identify, collect, and analyze the accumulated evidence. This is the approach we have adopted herein.

Another important aim of this book is to broaden the view of public area surveillance techniques beyond the current narrow focus on CCTV. There exist other forms of surveillance that may be equally if not more effective than CCTV, and they may impose fewer social costs on society. Put another way, surveillance for the purposes of preventing crime can be interpreted and implemented in many different ways. Policy makers would be well advised to consider the full range of available measures. In addition to CCTV, these include improved street lighting, security guards, place managers, and defensible space.

Briefly, place managers are persons such as bus drivers, parking lot attendants, train conductors, and others who perform a surveillance function by virtue of their position of employment. Unlike security personnel, however, the task of surveillance for these employees is secondary to other job duties. Defensible space involves design changes to the built environment to maximize the natural surveillance of open spaces (e.g., streets, parks) provided by people going about their day-to-day activities. Examples of design changes include the construction of street barricades or closures, redesign of walkways, and installation of windows. They can also include more mundane techniques, such as the removal of objects from shelves or windows of convenience stores that obscure lines of sight in the store and the removal or pruning of bushes in front of homes so that residents may have a clear view of the outside world.

Effectiveness in preventing crime—whether it is concerned with a narrow focus on CCTV or a broader, more complete focus that incorporates the full range of public area surveillance methods—is only one side of the story. It is important to investigate the potential social costs associated with public area surveillance methods and weigh these costs against any crime reduction benefits. Here, the question of interest is: How do we strike a balance between crime reduction and social costs? This is a matter that confronts many crime prevention policies, from early childhood intervention to reintegration of offenders into the community. It has particular salience with public area surveillance. This may be because of its increasingly widespread nature, perceived (or actual) permanency, and the unknown capabilities (Marx, 1988) of some of these methods.

The potential social costs of the different forms of surveillance range widely, from the seemingly mundane to the more serious that threaten personal protections and civil liberties. CCTV in public places often raises concerns over the invasion of privacy, threats to liberties, and contributing to a "fortress society." Also, as noted by Massachusetts Institute of Technology sociologist Gary Marx, "enthusiasm for the rapidly spreading, and minimally regulated, surveillance cameras needs to be tempered by awareness of their limitations," including the validity of the recorded image and the true meaning of images caught on camera (Marx, 2005). Some of the former concerns are also directed at security guards, including the view that these two methods of surveillance are further contributing to the social exclusion of some of society's most vulnerable members, such as the homeless, youths, and racial and ethnic minority groups. Street lighting, place managers, and most types of defensible space evoke far less resistance by the general public. Part of this stems from each of these being less intrusive, more benign forms of surveillance for preventing crime.

Key Results

On the basis of the highest quality research evidence available, a number of conclusions can be drawn about the specific conditions under which these surveillance measures are most effective in preventing crime in public places. Our reviews find that CCTV is effective in parking lots or car parks, improved street lighting is effective in city and town centers and residential/public housing communities, and the defensible space practice of street closures or barricades is effective in inner-city neighborhoods.

Also of importance is evidence showing that CCTV and improved street lighting are more effective in reducing property (and especially vehicle) crimes than in reducing violent crimes. Street closure or barricade schemes are effective in reducing both property and violent crimes. For security guards, the weight of the evidence suggests that they are promising when implemented in car parks and targeted at vehicle crimes. In contrast, place managers appear to be of unknown effectiveness in preventing crime. These less than conclusive statements about the effectiveness of security guards and places managers have everything to do with the small number of high-quality evaluations that have been carried out on these measures.

Analyses of the potential social costs associated with effective methods of public area surveillance produced the following conclusions. In the case of improved street lighting—the most effective of the surveillance techniques—the one potential drawback is that it may cause an increase in light pollution. For the defensible space practice of street closures or barricades in inner-city neighborhoods, by all accounts it, too, does not appear to cause any undue hardship to residents in these areas. However, other people are excluded. The only effective use of CCTV—when implemented in car parks and targeted at vehicle crimes—may also have few negative effects and arouse little resistance on the part of the general citizenry, at least compared to its use in other public settings. These other settings are where the CCTV debate heats up. On one hand, we conclude that CCTV is not very effective in preventing crime in city and town centers, public housing communities, and transportation facilities. On the other hand, in these areas the potential social costs are most troubling.

We also find that there is some evidence of the effectiveness of combining the different forms of public area surveillance. Perhaps it is time for policy makers, practitioners, and researchers to look more closely at how to maximize their shared effectiveness in reducing crime and capitalize on their different qualities. This seems to be particularly important in the effort to strive for the most effective and socially noninvasive use of surveillance to make public places safer from crime.

Public Area Surveillance

Each major form of public area surveillance is aimed at increasing offenders' perceptions of the risks associated with committing a crime. How these measures achieve this differs in some respects, and according to criminologists Derek Cornish and Ronald Clarke (2003), they can be grouped into three types of surveillance: formal surveillance, natural surveillance, and place managers (or surveillance by employees).

Formal surveillance aims to produce a "deterrent threat to potential offenders" (Clarke, 1997, p. 20) through the deployment of personnel whose primary responsibility is security (e.g., security guards) or through the introduction of some form of technology, such as CCTV, to enhance or take the place of security personnel. Place managers cover a wide range of employed persons who by virtue of their position (e.g., bus driver, parking lot attendant, train conductor) perform a secondary surveillance function.

Natural surveillance shares the same aim as formal surveillance, but involves efforts to "capitalize upon the 'natural' surveillance provided by people going about their everyday business" (Clarke, 1997, p. 21). Examples of natural surveillance include the installation or improvement of street lighting and defensible space measures.

As already noted, CCTV is the most popular of these surveillance techniques. Although some of this increased use has occurred in an effort to aid the police in the detection and prevention of terrorist activities, the prevention of crime remains an important aim of CCTV systems (Hauser, 2008).

In New Orleans, for example, the increase in crime, especially violent crime, following Hurricane Katrina has resulted in the implementation of the first wave of a large-scale CCTV project. Directed by the local police and prosecutor's office, CCTV is viewed as an important deterrent and investigatory tool to help curb crime in the city's high-crime areas (McCarthy, 2007). In contrast, New York City, which continues to have the lowest crime rate among all of the major U.S. cities and has even shown some reductions in serious crimes of late, has installed a large number of cameras in and around areas considered high-probability targets for terrorist activity (e.g., the subway system, the financial district, bridges). Crime prevention may be important here, but the detection and prevention of terrorist activities seems to be the top priority (Associated Press, 2006b).

Other widely used surveillance measures that perform a crime prevention function in public places include security guards, place managers, street lighting, and defensible space. In the United States today, the number of security guards, sometimes referred to as private police, far surpasses the number of publicly funded police officers. The growth in the use of security guards in public places, often to augment traditional policing services, shows no signs of slowing anytime soon (Sklansky, 2008). Place managers are also on the rise in the United States. There are signs that the secondary function of surveillance that these employees perform as part of their everyday duties is being given increased priority (Eck, 2006).

The natural surveillance techniques of improved street lighting and defensible space continue to hold a great deal of interest today as measures to reduce crime in public places. But they seemingly play more of a background role compared to some of the currently popular varieties of public area surveillance, especially CCTV. In many respects, street lighting has been integrated into the urban landscape. The need for improvements to and installation of lighting in high-crime areas remains a top priority. Defensible space practices have also been integrated into many public domains, and they have been particularly influential in the design of public housing communities.

We distinguish between public and private places. This book focuses on public area surveillance. By *public areas*, we mean those places that individuals can make use of or visit in a free and unencumbered way. Typical public places include city and town centers, public transportation facilities like subway systems, parking lots or car parks that are available for public use, public housing communities, public schools and universities, and government buildings.[1] Inevitably, there was some overlap between public and private places in a small number of studies included in our reviews. For example, an evaluation of a CCTV scheme in the London borough of Southwark (Sarno, Hough, and Bulos, 1999) included cameras that operated on city streets and a smaller number inside a private shopping center. Wherever possible, we restricted our analyses to the effects on crime in public places.

Our focus on making public places safer from crime is not meant to diminish the importance of efforts to reduce crime in private space. Instead, it allows for a more comprehensive examination of one aspect of the current debate on surveillance and crime prevention. This focus is also driven by the growing use of surveillance measures to reduce crime in public places.

In the following chapters we examine the critical dimensions of public area surveillance and crime prevention. Part I (chapters 2–4) focuses on the politics, theory, and methodology that are central to the study of public area surveillance and crime prevention. Part II (chapters 5–7) assesses the scientific evidence on the effectiveness of the major forms of surveillance that are designed to prevent crime in public places. Part III (chapters 8 and 9) explores policy choices and challenges and future directions in the use of these public area surveillance methods.

We hope this book will make a unique contribution to the debate on surveillance for crime prevention in public space by bringing together in one place the best available empirical evidence from evaluations about the effectiveness of these interventions in reducing crime.

Part I
Politics, Theory, and Method

The Politics of Surveillance for Crime Prevention

2

The use of surveillance measures to prevent crime in public places is no more influenced by the politics of the day than are efforts to assist offenders in returning to the community or measures to reduce gun violence. But public area surveillance measures, especially closed-circuit television (CCTV) cameras, by virtue of their intrusive nature (and growing prevalence) have raised the stakes on the political considerations that apply to their use in Western democracies. These political considerations may involve overlooking technological or human (in the case of security guards or CCTV operators, for example) limitations or casting aside the scientific evidence on alternative surveillance measures. In this political context, this chapter provides the background on the different forms of surveillance that are designed to prevent crime in public places.

Historical and Contemporary Developments

This section charts key historic and recent developments that have shaped the use of the major forms of surveillance to prevent crime in public places. It pays particular attention to the influence (or lack thereof) of research that has been carried out to investigate the impact that these forms of surveillance have had on crime.

Improved Street Lighting

Contemporary interest in the effect of improved street lighting on crime dates back to 1960s America, a time when crime rates were increasing dramatically.[1] Many towns and cities across the country embarked on major street lighting programs as a means of reducing crime, and initial results were encouraging (Wright, Heilweil, Pelletier, and Dickinson, 1974).

The proliferation of projects across the United States led to a detailed review of the effects of street lighting in preventing crime by James Tien and his colleagues (1979) as part of the National Evaluation Program of the Law Enforcement Assistance Administration (LEAA). Their report described how 103 street lighting projects that were originally identified were eventually reduced to a final sample of only 15 considered by the review team to contain sufficiently rigorous evaluative information.

With regard to the impact of street lighting on crime, Tien and colleagues (1979) found that the results were mixed and generally inconclusive. However, each project was considered seriously flawed because of such problems as weak design, misuse or absence of sound analytic techniques, inadequate measures of street lighting, poor measures of crime (all were based on police records), and insufficient appreciation of the impact of lighting on different types of crime.

Obviously, this review should have led to attempts to evaluate the effects of improved street lighting using more adequate designs and alternative measures of crime, such as victim surveys, self-reports, or systematic observation. It should also have stimulated efforts to determine in what circumstances improved street lighting might lead to reductions in crime. Unfortunately, it was interpreted as showing that street lighting had no effect on crime and effectively ended research on the topic in the United States for a long time.

Few crime prevention initiatives could have survived this rigorous examination unscathed. As Cambridge criminologist Kate Painter (1996, p. 318) noted:

> Despite the fact that other National Evaluations conducted
> at the same time (e.g., Operation Identification, Crime

Prevention Security Surveys, Citizen Patrols and Citizen Crime Reporting Projects) found evidence of programme impact to be inconsistent and inconclusive...all these strategies, with the exception of street lighting, continued to be promoted on both sides of the Atlantic. The reasons for ignoring the potential role of street lighting are difficult to determine.

In the United Kingdom, little research on street lighting and crime was conducted until the late 1980s (Fleming and Burrows, 1986). There was a resurgence of interest between 1988 and 1990, when three small-scale street lighting projects were implemented and evaluated in different areas of London: Edmonton, Tower Hamlets, and Hammersmith/Fulham (Painter, 1994). In each location, crime, disorder, and fear of crime declined, and pedestrian street use increased dramatically after the lighting improvements.

In contrast to these generally desirable results, a major British Home Office–funded evaluation in Wandsworth (Atkins, Husain, and Storey, 1991) concluded that improved street lighting had no effect on crime, and a Home Office review, published simultaneously, also asserted that "better lighting by itself has very little effect on crime" (Ramsay and Newton, 1991, p. 24). However, as further evidence accumulated, there were more signs that improved street lighting could have an effect in reducing crime. In a narrative review, British criminologist Ken Pease (1999, p. 68) considered that "the capacity of street lighting to influence crime has now been satisfactorily settled." He also recommended that the debate should be moved from the sterile "does it work or doesn't it?" to the more productive "how can I flexibly and imaginatively incorporate lighting in crime reduction strategy and tactics?" (p. 72).

Shortly following these pronouncements, the Home Office commissioned the first systematic review of the effects of improved street lighting on crime (Farrington and Welsh, 2002a; see also Farrington and Welsh, 2002b). From a meta-analysis of the studies included in the review (13 in total), we found that street lighting produced a significant and rather sizable (20%) reduction in crime.[2] The results were even more impressive for the five British studies included in the review, with a 30% reduction in crime. (The other eight studies were implemented in the United States.)

Little has changed in the United Kingdom since the release of these findings by the government in the summer of 2002. Street lighting improvement measures make up no part of the government's crime prevention policy, and to our knowledge no public funds have been expended on research in this area.

This abbreviated British story of street lighting and crime prevention contrasts starkly with the expansion of CCTV schemes in London and throughout the country. Indeed, the contemporary interest in contrasting these two situational crime prevention measures, as we did in an article in *Criminology and Public Policy* (Welsh and Farrington, 2004b), arises largely from the recent British experience of the widespread use of one of these measures (CCTV) as a government-funded method of preventing crime and the complete dismissal by the government of the other method (improved street lighting).

CCTV Cameras

The first use of CCTV cameras to prevent crime took place in the private sector (in retail in the United Kingdom and in banking in the United States), following the advent of video technology in the form of the videotape and VCR (video cassette recorder) in the 1960s. In the United States, the first documented use of public area CCTV occurred in the towns of Hoboken, New Jersey (in 1966), and Mount Vernon, New York (in 1971). In both cases, local police departments were responsible for monitoring the systems (Nieto, 1997, p. 14). In the United Kingdom, the earliest known public use of CCTV has been traced back to 1975, as part of an effort to deal with a surge in robberies and assaults on staff in the London Underground (McCahill and Norris, 2002, p. 8). CCTV was then deployed by the police throughout London to monitor "public order incidents and demonstrations"; by 1985, the first permanent public area system was installed in the town of Bournemouth (McCahill and Norris, 2002, pp. 8–9). It was not until 1994 that public area CCTV took on a prominent role in British government crime policy, with substantial funds allocated to local authorities (Williams and Johnstone, 2000, p. 188).

In recent years, there has been a marked and sustained growth in the use of CCTV surveillance cameras to prevent crime in public places in many Western nations. The United Kingdom in particular is on the cusp of becoming, in the words of some, a "surveillance society" (Goold, 2004; Norris, 2007; Norris and Armstrong, 1999). One estimate made in the early 2000s put the total number of public CCTV cameras in the United

Kingdom at 4.2 million, or one for every 14 citizens (Norris and McCahill, 2006), accounting for one-fifth of all CCTV cameras worldwide (Coleman, 2004). It has also been estimated that the average Briton is caught on camera 300 times each day (Associated Press, 2007).

There are no national estimates as yet on the number of CCTV cameras in the United States, but local accounts indicate that they are being installed at an unprecedented rate, and their popularity is not limited to large urban centers (Fountain, 2006; Nieto, Johnston-Dodds, and Simmons, 2002; Savage, 2007). Some of this increased use in the United States has come about in an effort to aid the police in the detection and prevention of terrorist activities, especially in New York City and other metropolises. However, the prevention of crime remains an important aim of these CCTV systems (Associated Press, 2006b; Hauser, 2008; Kinzer, 2004; McCarthy, 2007). Similar claims have been made in the United Kingdom about the purpose of public CCTV there (Associated Press, 2007). (See following discussion for more details on the application of CCTV to terrorism.)

There are signs that other countries, most more cautiously than the United Kingdom and United States, are increasingly experimenting with CCTV to prevent crime in public places. One source of this knowledge on the growth in public CCTV, limited but welcomed, comes in the form of evaluation research. In the course of the research for this book, we found evaluation studies of public CCTV schemes in a number of European countries, including Germany, Norway, and Sweden, as well as in Australia and Japan. Many of these countries have not previously used CCTV in public places, let alone evaluated its effects on crime.

The growth in CCTV has come with a huge price tag. In the United Kingdom, for example, CCTV has been and continues to be the single most heavily funded crime prevention measure operating outside of the criminal justice system. British criminologists Michael McCahill and Clive Norris (2002) estimate that more than £250 million (approximately $375 million as of this writing) of public money was spent on CCTV over the 10-year period of 1992 to 2002. This figure could very well be an underestimate. For example, between 1999 and 2001 alone, the British government made available £170 million (approximately $255 million) for "CCTV schemes in town and city centres, car parks, crime hot-spots and residential areas" (Home Office Policing and Reducing Crime Unit, 2001, p. 8). Over the past decade, CCTV accounted for more than three-quarters of total spending on crime prevention by the British Home Office (Koch, 1998; Reuters, 2007).

In the United States, public expenditures on CCTV range from $25 million for cameras in buses and subway stations in New York City to $5 million for a 2,000-camera system throughout Chicago's city center to more than $10 million in Baltimore (Associated Press, 2006a, 2006b; McCarthy, 2007).

During this time there has been much debate about the effectiveness of CCTV in preventing crime and hence on the wisdom of spending such large sums of money. A key issue is to what extent funding for CCTV, especially in the United Kingdom and United States, has been based on high-quality scientific evidence demonstrating its efficacy in preventing crime. Recent reviews that have examined the effectiveness of CCTV in preventing crime (Eck, 2006; Ratcliffe, 2006; Wilson and Sutton, 2003) have noted the need for higher quality, independent evaluation research.

To address some of these concerns with respect to the research in the United Kingdom, the British Home Office commissioned us to carry out the first systematic review of the effects of CCTV on crime in public space (Welsh and Farrington, 2002; see also Welsh and Farrington, 2003, 2004a, 2006b). Twenty-two evaluations met our inclusion criteria and were carried out in three public settings: city and town centers, public transport, and car parks. From a meta-analysis of those studies that provided the requisite data (19 in total), we found that CCTV produced a nonsignificant and rather small (8%) reduction in crime.[3] Of the three settings, CCTV was most effective in reducing crime in car parks, with a significant and sizable (41%) reduction. The effects of CCTV on crime in the other two settings were small and nonsignificant: city and town centers (7% reduction) and public transport (6% reduction). As with our improved street lighting research, the results of this review showed that CCTV systems in the United Kingdom seemed to be far more effective in preventing crime than those implemented in the United States. (We discuss possible reasons for this in chapter 5.)

A national evaluation of CCTV in the United Kingdom, headed by University of Leicester criminologist Martin Gill, soon followed (Gill and Spriggs, 2005; see also Farrington, Gill, Waples, and Argomaniz, 2007). Interestingly, the results of the national study were highly concordant with the results of our systematic review: CCTV had an overall small desirable effect on crime, was most effective in car parks, and had a marginal effect on crime in city and town centers (as well as in public housing).[4] Since this time, public CCTV schemes have continued to be established unabated in the United Kingdom, seemingly without attention to these research results.

Other Forms of Surveillance

Other widely used surveillance measures that perform a crime prevention function in public places include security guards, place managers, and defensible space. Unlike CCTV and improved street lighting, there does not appear to be an interesting, interwoven story line about the development of these other forms of surveillance. For sure, there is a great deal of overlap among the larger group of surveillance measures under discussion here. But apparently, security guards and place managers are more closely aligned with developments connected with modern public policing.

Security guards, sometimes referred to as private police, are the most widespread and recognizable of this category of other forms of surveillance to prevent crime in public places, and they represent a growth industry. Berkeley law professor David Alan Sklansky, who has studied private policing extensively, notes that people in the United States, especially those who are well off, have a greater chance of encountering a security guard than a police officer on any given day (2008, pp. 124–125).

In 1990 (apparently the most recent data available),[5] there were roughly 913,000 private security guards (a 10% increase in the past decade) and about 600,000 police in the United States. This means that for every two sworn police officers, there are three security guards, or a ratio of 1.5 to 1. Ten years earlier, the ratio of private police to public police was slightly less, at 1.4 to 1. As part of the research study that produced these estimates, projections were made up to 2000. Between 1990 and 2000, it was estimated that the ranks of security guards would grow by approximately 13%, to just over one million. With a slightly larger expected increase in public police (approximately 17%, from 600,000 to 700,000), which actually occurred, the ratio of private police to public police was predicted to remain at 1.5 to 1 (Cunningham, Strauchs, and Van Meter, 1990, pp. 185, 229).

Some of these security guards are employed to prevent crime in private places, but just how many is not known for sure. According to a survey by the Mercer Group (1997, as cited in Sklansky, 2006, p. 92), 45% of all local governments in the late 1990s contracted out some of their security work to private security firms, and an increasing amount of this work was devoted to patrols of government buildings, housing projects, and public parks.

This growth in security guards has also occurred in many other Western countries (Forst, 1999). In the United Kingdom, for example, the number of security guards increased by almost one-quarter (23%) between 1971 and 1991 (the latest data available). Unlike the United States, however, the ratio of security guards to police officers in the United Kingdom is much lower, at 1.1 to 1 (Wakefield, 2003).

Three main reasons have been advanced for the large increase in private policing in the past few decades in the United States (Sklansky, 1999). One is that private policing is part of a larger societal trend to privatize government services. Another is that there has been a large increase in what Canadian criminologists Clifford Shearing and Philip Stenning (1981) call "mass private property." These are privately owned places like shopping malls, office buildings, recreational facilities, and so on that are frequented by the public and have increasingly required protection from criminal activity above and beyond what public law enforcement is willing or able to provide. The third, what Sklansky (1999, p. 1222) calls the "most widespread explanation," is the "failure of public law enforcement to provide the amounts and kinds of policing that many people want." Similar reasons have been advanced for the growth in private policing in other Western nations (for the United Kingdom, see Jones and Newburn, 1998).

Despite the sustained growth in security guards and private policing more generally in the United States and other Western countries, little is known about their effectiveness in preventing crime in public places. University of Cincinnati criminologist John Eck's (2006) comprehensive review of what works in preventing crime at places contains to our knowledge the only assessment of the effects of security guards on crime in public space. He identified only five studies that evaluated the impact of adding security guards to parking lots. These produced mixed results in preventing vehicle crimes, leaving Eck to conclude that security guards are of "unknown effectiveness."

There are some signs that the use of place managers (Eck, 1995) such as bus drivers, parking lot attendants, train conductors, and others who perform a surveillance function by virtue of their position of employment, is also on the rise in the United States. The secondary function of surveillance that these employees perform as part of their everyday duties is seemingly taking on greater priority (Eck, 2006; Eck, Clarke, and Guerette, 2007). But little can be said about the effectiveness of this situational technique in the debate on preventing crime in public places. Disappointingly, Ronald Clarke and Gisela Bichler-Robertson's summary of the evaluation literature a decade ago seems equally applicable today: "there is little criminological research on the effectiveness of 'place managers' in preventing crime" (1998, p. 12). (We review the available research evidence in chapter 7.)

The beginnings of this form of surveillance to prevent crime in public places can largely be traced to Europe. In the United Kingdom, the Department of the Environment implemented some of the first programs on public housing estates in the 1970s. Resident caretakers were employed to maintain the buildings and grounds, assist residents with needs related to their flats, and serve as a visible presence on the estate (Hough, Clarke, and Mayhew, 1980). In the Netherlands, "occupational surveillance" or surveillance by employees became an important component of government crime prevention policy in the 1980s, with initiatives dating back to the 1960s. These have included adding more inspectors on the metro, trams, and buses; introducing caretakers to council estates (public housing communities); and implementing a program of *Stadswacht* or city guards to patrol city streets. The city guards and many of the other people who are hired and trained to perform these tasks are often drawn from the long-term unemployed (van Dijk, 1995). The initial government funding for the public transport inspectors (also known as VICs or "safety, information and control" officers) was for hiring young people, most of whom were unemployed (van Andel, 1989).

Although more difficult to gauge than security guards and place managers, the use of the natural surveillance technique of defensible space to prevent crime in public places is still of interest. Coined by the American architect Oscar Newman (1972), defensible space involves design changes to the built environment to maximize the natural surveillance of open spaces (e.g., streets, parks, parking lots) provided by people going about their day-to-day activities. First implemented in public housing projects, one of its applications was to redesign buildings to allow "residents a better view of vulnerable areas" (Hough, Clarke, and Mayhew, 1980, p. 8). Rutgers University criminologist Ronald Clarke (1997, p. 8) notes that Newman's concept of defensible space has influenced the design of public housing communities across the world.

Media Influences

More so than any of the other forms of surveillance covered in this book, the media's influence in shaping public and political support has been most evident with respect to CCTV in the United Kingdom. This has come about in large measure because of TV news shows and other programs broadcasting images of suspected offenders and sometimes criminal acts that have been captured by video surveillance cameras. Often these images are aired shortly following the event. Sometimes the police release the video to enlist the public's assistance in the apprehension of the suspect, to help in identifying the victim's whereabouts, or both. Not surprisingly, the images also make for gripping television, showing the gritty and sometimes tragic reality of crime. Often played over and over, as well as shown on the Internet and in the print media, these images can have a profound effect on the viewing audience.

This was certainly true in the case of the abduction of the British toddler James Bulger, perhaps the most influential event caught on a CCTV camera. On February 12, 1993, the two-year-old was abducted from a shopping mall in the northern town of Bootle, Merseyside, not far from Liverpool. James's mother stopped to look at a display window of one of the stores, letting go of his hand for a few moments. When she turned around, her son was gone. The whole event was caught on the mall's video surveillance system. The grainy video, later played on the national news and around the world, showed two schoolboys, 10-year-olds Jon Venables and Robert Thompson, walking up to James and calmly leading him out of the mall. The child's badly beaten body was found a short time later near railway tracks, a short distance from the mall. Because of the video, along with the boys' boasting to their friends, the two were quickly apprehended and taken into custody. The video evidence also helped secure guilty pleas from the two boys.

Social scientists and social commentators alike have remarked how this was a singular event that catapulted public support for and swept away any lingering signs of political resistance to CCTV throughout the United Kingdom (McCahill and Norris, 2002; Norris and McCahill, 2006;

Parenti, 2003). This led to the first major expansion of open-street or public area CCTV systems in the country (Norris and McCahill, 2006, p. 100). For sure, the conditions in favor of the expansion of public CCTV were building prior to this event. The most notable of these included the dramatic increase in crime rates and the need to augment what was viewed as an ineffective criminal justice response, especially on the part of the police. But the images depicted on the screen of the older boys leading James Bulger away from his mother, coupled with the discovery of his beaten body, tipped the scales in favor of CCTV. As noted by McCahill and Norris (2002, p. 12), "The public mood in the wake of the killing, as evidenced by the newspapers of the time, made those who tried to raise objections to CCTV seem either callous or too concerned with the rights of criminals."

What if any residual effect this may have had on the American public's support for the use of CCTV in public places is not known. However, there has been no shortage of equally predatory and tragic events caught on video and viewed by the public in this country. In the absence of research on the topic, it is conceivable that such events may have contributed to the lack of public and political resistance to the growth of public area CCTV surveillance that is presently occurring in the U.S.

Social Costs

The potential social costs of the different forms of surveillance covered in this book are wide-ranging. By now the reader will be able to say with some accuracy where these different forms of surveillance fall on this continuum of social costs. Arguably, improved street lighting and defensible space have few (if any) social costs. CCTV, on the other hand, raises a number of pressing social concerns, and security guards and place managers fall somewhere in the middle of this continuum. Whatever the case may be, these costs, among other matters of public interest, need to be weighed against any crime prevention benefits that may accrue from the different forms of surveillance.

In many respects, as Cambridge criminologist Andrew von Hirsch (2000) argues in the context of public area CCTV, there are two major issues in discussing the "proper uses and limits" of surveillance measures. First, there is the matter of privacy concerns. For our purposes, this is broadened to include other social costs that may infringe on public interests or even violate legal or constitutional protections. This is the subject of this section. Second, there is the matter of the legitimizing role of crime prevention, or as von Hirsch (2000, p. 61) posits, "To what extent does crime prevention legitimise impinging on any interests of privacy or anonymity in public space?" This is a subject we take up in chapter 8, where we discuss policy choices and challenges that confront surveillance for crime prevention in public places.

As one of the main crime prevention strategies (Tonry and Farrington, 1995b), situational crime prevention is often singled out as having more than its share of potential harmful social consequences. Some of the most important social harms associated with situational prevention include: displacement of crime to other areas or an escalation in crime severity; reinforcement of the notion of a fortress society; exclusion of so-called undesirables from public places; threats to civil liberties; an increased regimentation of society; and the promotion of victim blaming (Clarke, 2000, pp. 101–107). Not all of these potential social harms have relevance to the situational surveillance measures that we discuss here. Moreover, Ronald Clarke (2000; see also Felson and Clarke, 1997) notes that situational crime prevention in general has been unfairly judged because many of these social harms apply only to highly specific situational measures, and other harms are misconstrued, such as victim blaming (i.e., by pointing out the risks to potential victims from not taking certain precautions).

Displacement—the phenomenon of crime being displaced to adjacent, nontargeted areas, increasing in seriousness, and taking other forms—is a potential social harm that is associated with CCTV, improved street lighting, and other forms of surveillance. In fact, all situational prevention measures could conceivably lead to the displacement of crime in one form or another, especially on spatial or temporal dimensions. This being said, it is more difficult to conceive how these surveillance measures could result in an escalation in crime severity, as in the case of a pickpocket turning to mugging. Usually, displacement follows from target hardening (e.g., the installation of locks or physical barriers) and other situational measures that attempt to increase the perceived effort required to commit a crime. What Clarke (1995b) and many others (Gabor, 1990; Hesseling, 1994) have found and rightly note is that displacement is never 100%. Furthermore, a growing body of research has shown that situational measures may instead result in a diffusion of crime prevention benefits or the complete opposite of displacement (Clarke and Weisburd, 1994). Benefits may be diffused to surrounding areas that are not targeted by the intervention. Similar results have been found for hot-spot policing interventions (Braga, 2006; Weisburd et al., 2006). (We discuss displacement and diffusion effects in more detail in the context of evidence-based crime prevention in chapter 4.)

Public area CCTV is most closely associated with concerns over threats to civil liberties, including the invasion of privacy. The right to privacy in public settings can be construed as an ordinary person (behaving in an ordinary way) having an expectation of remaining anonymous, that is, "to be able to go about without being identified, and without having their activities subjected to special or prolonged scrutiny" (von Hirsch, 2000, pp. 61–62). Some contend that public CCTV infringes on this basic right.

In the United States, the concept of privacy is perhaps best recognized in the constitutional guarantee to be free from government intrusions found in the Fourth Amendment, and the most commonly identified challenge to the government's use of public video surveillance is that it violates the Fourth Amendment's prohibition against "unreasonable searches and seizures." The American Civil Liberties Union claims that the general use of video surveillance to monitor the movement of people in public places, without a search warrant, constitutes an unreasonable search (Stanley and Steinhardt, 2003). Although the Fourth Amendment as applied to the use of public area CCTV has not yet been tested in the U.S. Supreme Court, Marcus Nieto and his colleagues (2002, p. 38) note that "the prevailing view has been that video surveillance does not violate the Fourth Amendment."

Public video surveillance has also been interpreted by some to be a violation of an individual's First Amendment rights. Continuous public video surveillance is seen as a form of intimidation, creating a "chilling effect" on free speech activity. It is argued that the presence of cameras has the potential to provide a chilling effect on legal behavior (Nguyen, 2002). This may create a fear of speaking out or participating in constitutionally protected acts such as civil rights marches, rallies, and so on. This form of surveillance is considered by many to be a form of harassment. Likewise, the right to free association may be compromised by the use of CCTV in public places.

CCTV cameras may also give the appearance of contributing to "a harsh, uncaring fortress society" (Clarke, 2000, p. 102). The notion of a fortress society is most closely associated with gated communities, which are areas characterized by a secure perimeter in the form of gates or walls that deny access to nonresidents. Video surveillance is sometimes used to enhance access control, as well as to create a deterrent threat around the perimeter, and it may be supplemented by security guards.

The use of CCTV cameras, as well as security guards, in public places have also been criticized on the grounds that they may result in the social exclusion of, in the words of Clarke (2000, p. 104), "so-called 'undesirables' (vagrants, the homeless, minorities and unemployed young people)." Similar to gated communities, these measures are seen as further contributing to the divide that exists between society's haves and have-nots.

One could certainly take issue with the increased use of place managers in public settings, viewing them as yet another set of eyes that are watching both potential offenders and mild-mannered citizens alike. Unlike security guards, surveillance is not the primary function of place managers. In this regard, the use of place managers may strike a fairly good balance between the public's interest in community safety and concerns over the erosion of privacy and civil liberties.

Improved street lighting, by almost all accounts, presents no harmful social consequences. It does not violate anyone's privacy, infringe on civil liberties, or contribute to the social exclusion of groups. It may be deemed a nonthreatening form of natural surveillance to aid in the prevention of crime, among its other uses. In many respects, the same can be said about defensible space, another form of natural surveillance that is intended to improve lines of sight to take advantage of the surveillance capabilities of passersby and others living and working in proximity to public places.

To our knowledge, the one potential social harm associated with improved street lighting is that it may contribute to light pollution (Pease, 1999). This was brought to our attention after the publication of our first systematic review on the subject (Farrington and Welsh, 2002a, 2002b). The International Dark Skies Association, a group of professional and amateur astronomers who advocate the elimination of outdoor lighting so as not to interfere with nighttime viewing of the skies, critiqued our work through one of its supporters in a couple of journal articles (Marchant, 2004, 2005; for rebuttals, see Farrington and Welsh, 2004, 2006b). We do not deny that improved street lighting may cause an increase in light pollution and make it harder to view the skies, and it is a potential cost that should be considered in decisions to implement lighting schemes. However, certain modern types of lighting are designed to shine downward rather than upward, thus minimizing light pollution. For many, especially those who live in urban areas, light pollution may be a small price to pay for the crime reduction benefits that have been shown to accrue from lighting improvements.

Applications to Terrorism

CCTV and security guards are especially relevant in the detection and prevention of terrorist acts. Indeed, for the police the potential benefit of CCTV in reducing crime—by deterring offenders from committing illegal activities—may be much lower on the list of priorities than the prevention of terrorist activities, whether through the identification of suspicious persons or packages or to aid in the identification, apprehension, and conviction of suspects after the act.

The role of CCTV in counterterrorism has played a major part in garnering public and political support for its widespread implementation in public settings throughout the United Kingdom (McCahill and Norris, 2002; Parenti, 2003; Rosen, 2001). The Irish Republican Army's terrorist attack on Bishopgate in 1993 is seen as "the original catalyst for CCTV expansion" in central London. This led to the introduction of the Ring of Steel, a network of cameras used to monitor the many entrances to the City of London (Norris and McCahill, 2006, p. 101). While some referred to it more playfully as the Ring of Plastic because of its use of plastic markers to guide traffic through the city, Ronald Clarke and Graeme Newman (2006, p. 173) note that by the late 1990s the CCTV component of the Ring of Steel was recording the license plate of every vehicle that entered London.

The role of CCTV in counterterrorism was further emphasized in the suicide bombings carried out in London's transportation system on July 7, 2005. Four separate explosions on trains in the London Underground (the Tube) and aboard a double-decker bus resulted in 52 deaths and more than 700 injuries among passengers; the four suicide bombers also died. CCTV video footage, viewed days later by police and counterterrorism authorities, captured four young men with identical large military-style backpacks or rucksacks leaving King's Cross station during the morning rush hour (Campbell and Laville, 2005). The investigation later revealed that CCTV cameras had filmed three of the four suicide bombers carrying out a dry run of their attack nine days earlier. The authorities reported that the men carried rucksacks identical to those used on the day of the bombings and spent three hours in London "checking times and security around an area between King's Cross and Baker Street" (Steele, 2005).

Although the CCTV cameras did not prevent the terrorist acts, the images of the suicide bombers proved vital to the investigation and have since played a role in improving counterterrorism measures in London's vast public transportation system. One immediate benefit of the images and the subsequent identification of the perpetrators is that it allowed police to trace their movements on the day (with the aid of even more CCTV images) and identify their points of origin. This led police to discover a car at another railway station with a "ready to go" bomb and bomb-making equipment as well as a property in Leeds where the bombs were made (Steele, 2005).

Similarly, in the United States, the terrorist acts perpetrated on September 11, 2001, have contributed to an increased use of public CCTV in this country (Clymer, 2002; Murphy, 2002). In New York City, a large number of cameras have been installed in and around areas considered high-probability targets for terrorist activity (e.g., the subway system, bridges, the financial district). As already noted, crime prevention may be important here, but the detection and prevention of terrorist activities is apparently the top priority.

The threat of future terrorist acts has also contributed to an increase in security guards in the United States. University of California at Davis law professor Elizabeth Joh (2004, p. 49) contends that private police are the "first line of defense in the post September 11th world." It can also be surmised that this has influenced to some degree the present growth in certain place managers like subway and bus conductors.

Conclusions

Perhaps not surprisingly, scientific evidence has not figured prominently (or at all) in decisions to implement surveillance measures designed to prevent crime in public places. This is most evident in the case of CCTV. The popularization of CCTV, at least in the United Kingdom, also had the effect of casting aside the scientific evidence on alternative surveillance measures. Street lighting was one of these. To be sure, the issue here was not about choosing one method over the other (they often complement one another) but about giving serious consideration to the research evidence of the day. In the case of other public area surveillance measures, little can be said about how they have figured in the debate on preventing crime in public places. This is certainly true for place managers and may also be true for defensible space. The problem here is too few evaluations or no systematic assessment of the existing evaluation research. (In chapter 7, we attempt to rectify this by carrying out systematic reviews of all three of the other forms of crime prevention surveillance measures.) Security guards, on the other hand, are a well-established surveillance method in preventing crime and are seemingly becoming even more prevalent in public areas.

A number of other important issues have shaped political and policy decisions on public area surveillance and crime prevention. In the United Kingdom, the television media—through the depiction of criminal events caught on camera—have had an effect in galvanizing support for the widespread use of CCTV. This began with the tragic case of James Bulger and has continued to this day with the broadcast of images (after the fact) of suicide bombers entering the London Underground. It is conceivable that equally predatory and tragic events caught on tape and viewed by the American public may lend support to the growth of public area CCTV surveillance in this country.

Another issue of political and policy significance is the potential social costs associated with public area surveillance. Each of the surveillance measures described here may result in some social costs, ranging from the mundane to the more serious that threaten personal protections and liberties. For street lighting and defensible space, the social costs may be fairly minor, whereas for CCTV and security guards, the stakes appear to be much higher. Displacement of crime is one social cost that can potentially affect every method of public area surveillance. However, this may be countered by the very real (and well-documented) effect that instead of displacing crime, these measures may produce unintended crime prevention benefits in adjacent areas not targeted by the intervention or after the intervention has ended.

Still another issue of great interest is that some of these public area surveillance measures are also highly relevant to current efforts to detect and prevent domestic terrorism. The role of CCTV and, perhaps to a lesser extent, security guards in counterterrorism has played an important part in garnering support for their widespread use in some Western countries.

That these and other public area surveillance measures may produce benefits beyond crime reduction is of particular interest to all concerned parties, and we return to this issue in chapter 8.

In the next chapter, we discuss the leading theories and perspectives that have been advanced to explain how the different methods of public area surveillance might reduce crime.

How Might Surveillance
Measures Reduce
Crime?

In the parlance of criminology, the major forms of public area surveillance are commonly categorized under the heading of situational crime prevention, which refers to interventions designed to prevent the occurrence of crimes by reducing the opportunities and increasing the risk and difficulty of offending. Rutgers University criminologist Ronald Clarke (1995b, 1997) is one of the pioneers of situational crime prevention, which is considered one of the four major strategies of reducing crime (Tonry and Farrington, 1995b). The other three are developmental, community, and criminal justice prevention. *Developmental prevention* refers to interventions designed to prevent the development of criminal potential in individuals, especially those methods targeting risk and protective factors discovered in studies of human development (Farrington and Welsh, 2007; Tremblay and Craig, 1995). *Community prevention* refers to interventions designed to change the social conditions and institutions (e.g., families, peers, social norms, clubs, organizations) that influence offending in residential communities (Hope, 1995). *Criminal justice prevention* refers to traditional deterrent, incapacitative, and rehabilitative strategies operated by law enforcement and criminal justice system agencies (Blumstein, Cohen, and Nagin, 1978; MacKenzie, 2006).

Situational prevention stands apart from these other strategies by its singular focus on the setting or place in which criminal acts take place as well as its crime-specific focus. Related to this is the widely held finding that crime is not randomly distributed across a city or community but is instead highly concentrated in certain places, which Cambridge University criminologist Lawrence Sherman has called crime "hot spots" (Sherman, Gartin, and Buerger, 1989). In the same way that individuals can have criminal careers, there are also criminal careers of places (Sherman, 1995).

Criminologists Derek Cornish and Ronald Clarke (2003), in their classification of situational crime prevention, differentiate three types of surveillance, each aimed primarily at increasing offenders' perceived risks of committing a crime: formal surveillance, natural surveillance, and place managers (or surveillance by employees).[1]

Explanations of the way these different forms of surveillance can reduce crime can be grouped into two main perspectives. One perspective is that of situational crime prevention. This may be viewed as having a specific effect on crime. It is also possible that these different forms of surveillance could reduce crime by strengthening informal social control and community cohesion, by improving the physical environment and greater investment in neighborhood conditions (Taub, Taylor, and Dunham, 1984; Taylor and Gottfredson, 1986). This approach may be viewed as having a more general effect on crime.

Situational Crime Prevention

Situational crime prevention is defined as "a preventive approach that relies, not upon improving society or its institutions, but simply upon reducing opportunities for crime" (Clarke, 1992, p. 3). Reducing opportunities for crime is achieved essentially through some modification or manipulation of the physical environment in order to directly affect offenders' perceptions of increased risks and effort and decreased rewards.

The theoretical origins of situational crime prevention are wide-ranging (see Garland, 2000; Newman, Clarke, and Shoham, 1997), but it is largely informed by opportunity theory. This theory holds that the offender is "heavily influenced by environmental inducements and opportunities and as being highly adaptable to changes in the situation" (Clarke, 1995a, p. 57). Opportunity theory includes several more specific theories. One of these is the rational choice perspective. This perspective appears to have had the greatest influence on the pragmatic orientation of situational crime prevention, as articulated by its chief architect, Ronald Clarke (1995a, 1995b, 1997). For this reason, it is the main focus here.

Three main components make up the rational choice perspective: (1) the image of a reasoning offender, (2) a crime-specific focus, and (3) the development of separate models for the decision to commit a crime and the choice of the target (Cornish and Clarke, 1986, p. 7). The image of a reasoning offender is understood to mean that

> crime is purposive behavior designed to meet the offender's commonplace needs for such things as money, status, sex, and excitement, and that meeting these needs involves the making of (sometimes quite rudimentary) decisions and choices, constrained as these are by limits of time and ability and the availability of relevant information. (Clarke, 1995b, p. 98)

On the basis of this view, it is assumed that rationality is not limited to offending behavior of a less serious nature (e.g., property crime) but is also present in violent offending. However, British psychologist Gordon Trasler (1986, 1993) argued that opportunity-reducing prevention is effective only with "instrumental" offenses (i.e., property, including robbery), not with "expressive" offenses. The examples given by Trasler (1993, p. 318) for expressive crimes were homicide or wounding, where, in his words, "the notion of a rational calculus was unconvincing." The empirical literature on the subject, albeit limited, suggests that situational crime prevention can be effective in reducing some violent crimes (see Eck, 2006). Similarly, it has been argued that situational prevention is most effective with casual, uncommitted offenders and least effective with persistent or chronic offenders (Trasler, 1986, 1993).

The crime-specific focus of the rational choice perspective is driven by its concern with environmental influences and criminal events. The adoption of a crime-specific focus is important to take account of the different decision processes and information used for the many different offenses (Clarke, 1995b). This focus ensures that the scope of intervention is not limited to the commonplace distinctions between crimes (e.g., residential or commercial burglary) but takes into account even the smallest variations.

In contrast, most other criminological theories assume that offenders are versatile and that it is unnecessary to propose a different theory for every different type of crime. For example, developmental and life-course theories aim to explain why offenders develop rather than why offenses occur. Put another way, they aim to explain the development of a potential for offending rather than how the potential becomes the actuality in any given situation. However, theories have been proposed that include both approaches and address both questions (Farrington, 2005). A crime-specific focus seems more necessary in explaining immediate situational influences on criminal acts rather than explaining the development of a more general tendency to commit offenses.

The final main component of the rational choice perspective on criminal behavior is the view that the decision processes involved in choosing the criminal event (the target) are equally important to the decision processes surrounding criminal involvement (deciding to offend). However, situational prevention concentrates on the event, because decisions are easier to influence at this stage. Event decisions take place in the present and depend on immediate circumstances and situations (Clarke, 1995b; Cornish and Clarke, 1986).

The situational approach is also supported by theories that emphasize natural, informal surveillance as a key to crime prevention. For example, Jane Jacobs (1961) drew attention to the role of good visibility combined with natural surveillance as deterrents to crime. She emphasized the association between levels of crime and public street use, suggesting that less crime would be committed in areas with an abundance of potential witnesses.

Lighting improvements, for instance, may encourage increased street usage, which intensifies natural surveillance. The change in routine activity patterns works to reduce crime because it increases the flow of potentially capable guardians who can intervene to prevent crime (Cohen and Felson, 1979). From a potential offender's perspective, the proximity of other pedestrians acts as a deterrent because the risks of being recognized or interrupted when attacking personal or property targets are increased. From a potential victim's perspective, the perceived risks and fears of crime are reduced.

A more classical situational perspective suggests that closed-circuit television (CCTV) (especially if well publicized), security personnel, and place managers may prevent crime because potential offenders are deterred by their increased subjective probability of being detected. These forms of surveillance may also increase the true probability of detection.

British criminologists Rachel Armitage, Graham Smyth, and Ken Pease (1999, p. 226) refer to this mechanism as "you've been framed." In the context of CCTV, the authors identify a number of other mechanisms by which it (as well as other surveillance measures) may prevent crime, including:

a. Effective deployment: CCTV directs security personnel to ambiguous situations, which may head off their translation into real criminal acts.

b. Publicity: CCTV could symbolize efforts to take crime seriously, and the perception of those efforts may energize law-abiding citizens and/or deter others.

c. Time for crime: CCTV may be perceived as reducing the time available to commit crime, preventing those crimes that require extended time and effort.

d. Memory jogging: the presence of CCTV may induce people to take elementary security precautions, such as locking their car, by jogging their memory about the possibility of being victimized.

e. Anticipated shaming: the presence of CCTV may induce people to take elementary security precautions, for fear that they will be shamed by being shown on CCTV as being careless.

f. Appeal to the cautious: cautious people migrate to the areas containing CCTV to shop, leave their cars, and so on. Their caution and security-mindedness reduce the risk of victimization. (Armitage, Smyth, and Pease, 1999, p. 227)

Natural surveillance, such as lighting and defensible space, may reduce crime by improving visibility. This deters potential offenders by increasing the risks that they will be recognized or interrupted in the course of their activities (Mayhew et al., 1979). Armitage and her colleagues (1999, p. 226) refer to this mechanism as "caught in the act." Security personnel and place managers also act as visible deterrents.

In addition, enhanced visibility and increased street usage may interact to heighten possibilities for informal surveillance. Pedestrian density and flow and surveillance have long been regarded as crucial for crime control since they can influence potential offenders' perceptions of the likely risks of being caught (Bennett and Wright, 1984; Newman, 1972). Or, to take a more colloquial expression, this is the "nosy parker" syndrome at work: more people frequenting the watched-over place, thus increasing the extent of natural surveillance by these "newcomers" to deter potential offenders (Armitage, Smyth, and Pease, 1999, pp. 226–227).

Problem-Oriented Policing

One particularly noteworthy influence on situational prevention has been the policing strategy known as problem-oriented policing (POP), pioneered by Herman Goldstein (1979, 1990). Indeed, Ronald Clarke (2007) notes that the development of situational prevention is very closely tied to POP.

POP is best described as an approach that is concerned with responding not to criminal incidents but to the underlying problems that give rise to the incidents. In the words of Harvard University criminologist Mark Moore (1992, p. 120), "This is not the same as seeking out the root causes of the crime problem in general. It is a much shallower, more situational approach."

Both POP and situational prevention are founded on similar models for guiding the implementation of programs. In the case of POP, officers follow a four-step problem-solving model that has come to be known as SARA, for Scanning, Analysis, Response, and Assessment. In situational crime prevention, an action-research model guides the process from analysis through assessment. One key difference between the concepts is that unlike situational prevention, POP is not exclusively focused on crime; it is also concerned with quality of life matters—in as much as these could be factors contributing to crime problems. Another important difference is that POP is primarily a police management approach, whereas situational prevention "can be utilized within any organizational or management structure and is open, not just to the police, but to whoever can muster the resources to tackle the problem at hand" (Clarke, 1997, p. 9).

Even more important than the similarities and differences that exist between situational prevention and POP is their shared focus on highly innovative and creative ways to reduce crime, as Harvard University criminologist Anthony Braga (2008) pointed out. This is a hallmark of both approaches and in many respects sets them apart from other crime prevention strategies and policing tactics.

Community Investment

Other theoretical perspectives have emphasized the importance of investment to improve neighborhood conditions as a means of strengthening community confidence, cohesion, and social control. This approach is sometimes called community crime prevention. However, this broad, organizing view is of limited utility, largely because there is little agreement on the definition of *community crime prevention* and the programs that fall within in it (Bennett, 1998). More useful is British criminologist Trevor Bennett's (1998) delineation of the main theories that have come to inform community crime prevention programs. In the present context of surveillance for crime prevention in public space, two theories are most applicable: social (or community) disorganization and community disorder.

Social disorganization theory attributes crime and disorder in a community to poor neighborhood controls. According to criminologists Robert Bursik and Harold Grasmick (1993), the most important causes of social or community disorganization are poverty, high residential mobility, racial or ethnic heterogeneity, and high population density. These factors lead to poor neighborhood controls, including poor supervision and surveillance by the residents, and a low willingness to intervene to prevent crime and disorder. In socially disorganized neighborhoods, there are weak ties between residents, few social networks, a low consensus on values and norms, and low community interaction and shared obligations.

Robert Sampson, Stephen Raudenbush, and Felton Earls (1997) argued that a low degree of "collective efficacy" in a neighborhood (a low degree of informal social control) causes high crime rates. This more contemporary view of community or social disorganization theory stresses the importance of structural influences on offending, such as family disruption and weak social cohesion.[2] Important to the construct of weak social control is an unwillingness of neighbors to intervene on behalf of the "common good."

Under the general framework of community disorganization theory, the scope for the prevention of crime, at least during the first half of the twentieth century, was seen to rest "in a program of the physical rehabilitation of slum areas and the development of community organization" (Burgess, 1942, p. xi). In more recent decades, community disorganization theory has given rise to programs emphasizing the empowerment or mobilization of community residents to take preventive action to reduce crime in their neighborhoods (Rosenbaum, Lurigio, and Davis, 1998).

Community disorder theory has its roots in the Broken Windows hypothesis of James Q. Wilson and George Kelling (1982; see also Kelling and Coles, 1996). Here, it is believed that improved neighborhood conditions will result from a specific focus on social and physical disorder (Skogan, 1990). This view postulates that disorder is a precursor to more serious street crime and decay by engendering fear among community members and producing a spiral of decline and weakened social control.[3] The scope for crime prevention rests largely on tackling disorderly behavior when it is minor, the precursor conditions that encourage such behavior to take root in the community, or both. Failing to repair the figurative and literal broken window signals that an area is deteriorating, and this encourages further disorder, whereas intervening early to repair the broken window prevents this view (and its consequences) developing.

As highly visible signs of investment, CCTV and improved street lighting might reduce crime if they were perceived to improve the environment and signal to residents that efforts were being made to invest in the neighborhood. In turn, this might lead residents to have a more positive image of their area and increased community pride, optimism, and cohesion. This might lead residents to exert greater informal social control over potential offenders in an area, even going so far as to intervene on behalf of their neighbors or for the common good. Note that increased social control and community cohesion should cause a reduction in both daytime and nighttime crime. Consequently, attempts to measure the effects of improved street lighting on crime should not concentrate purely on nighttime crime. The same holds true for evaluations of CCTV because infrared and other night-vision technology can allow CCTV to operate just as effectively at night as during the day.

In addition, the renovation of a highly noticeable component of the physical environment combined with changed social dynamics may act as a psychological deterrent against crime. Potential offenders may judge that the image of the location is improving and that social control, order, and surveillance are increasing (Taylor and Gottfredson, 1986). In the case of improved lighting, they may deduce that crime in the relit location is riskier than elsewhere, and this can influence their behavior in two ways. First, potential offenders living in this area may be deterred from committing offenses or escalating activities in this area. Second, potential offenders living outside the area may be deterred from entering it to commit crimes (Kelling and Coles, 1996; Wilson and Kelling, 1982).

Other Considerations

It is important to acknowledge that these surveillance measures might also cause crime to increase. Let us take CCTV as an example. The visible presence of the cameras could give potential victims a false sense of security and make them more vulnerable if they relax their vigilance or stop taking precautions such as walking in groups at night and not wearing expensive jewelry. CCTV may also encourage increased reporting of crimes to the police and increased recording of crimes by the police. If an offender is detected through CCTV, the offense may be recorded and detected at the same time, leading to an increase in police clearance rates as well as in crime rates. Hence, to disentangle criminal behavior from reporting and recording, both surveys and recorded crime measures are needed in any evaluation. As discussed in chapter 2, CCTV and other surveillance measures may also cause crime to be displaced to other locations, times, or victims.

In the case of street lighting improvements, they could, in certain circumstances, increase opportunities for crime. They may bring a greater number of potential victims and offenders into the same physical space. Increased visibility of possible victims may allow potential offenders to make better judgments of their vulnerability and attractiveness as a target (e.g., in terms of valuables). Increased social activity outside the home may increase the number of unoccupied homes available for burglary. Increased illumination may make it easier for offenders to commit crimes and escape.

The effects of each of the surveillance methods are also likely to vary in different conditions. Again, considering street lighting improvements, the effects are likely to be greater if the existing lighting is poor and if the improvement is considerable. Furthermore, the effects may vary according to characteristics of the area or the residents, the design of the area, the design of the lighting, and the places that are illuminated. For example, improved lighting may increase community confidence only in relatively stable, homogenous communities, not in areas with a heterogeneous population mix and high residential mobility. The effects of improved lighting may also interact with other environmental improvements, such as CCTV cameras, security patrols, place managers, or changes to the built environment. In particular, CCTV may be more effective in combination with improved lighting. Improved street lighting may have different effects on different types of crimes (e.g., violence versus property) and different effects on daytime as opposed to nighttime crime.

Conclusions

The relationship among visibility, social surveillance, and criminal opportunities is a consistently strong theme emerging from the literature. A core assumption of both opportunity and informal social control models of prevention is that criminal opportunities and risks are influenced by environmental conditions in interaction with resident and offender characteristics. Street lighting, CCTV, and some physical design changes to buildings and parks, for example, are tangible alterations to the built environment, but they do not constitute a physical barrier to crime. However, they, along with other forms of surveillance, can act as a catalyst to stimulate crime reduction through a change in perceptions, attitudes, and behavior of residents and potential offenders.

Based on these theoretical perspectives, the ways that CCTV, street lighting, security guards, and other forms of surveillance can prevent crime share a number of commonalities. Of course, there are some differences among these types of surveillance. One such difference rests on the widely held perception that CCTV is much more threatening to the civil liberties of law-abiding citizens (Clarke, 2000). This is a topic we return to in the last two chapters.

In the next chapter, we discuss the methods used in the evidence-based approach to evaluating the effectiveness of crime prevention measures.

Evidence-Based Crime Prevention

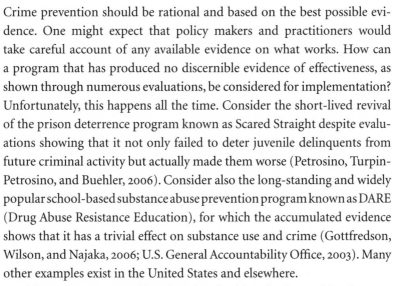

Crime prevention should be rational and based on the best possible evidence. One might expect that policy makers and practitioners would take careful account of any available evidence on what works. How can a program that has produced no discernible evidence of effectiveness, as shown through numerous evaluations, be considered for implementation? Unfortunately, this happens all the time. Consider the short-lived revival of the prison deterrence program known as Scared Straight despite evaluations showing that it not only failed to deter juvenile delinquents from future criminal activity but actually made them worse (Petrosino, Turpin-Petrosino, and Buehler, 2006). Consider also the long-standing and widely popular school-based substance abuse prevention program known as DARE (Drug Abuse Resistance Education), for which the accumulated evidence shows that it has a trivial effect on substance use and crime (Gottfredson, Wilson, and Najaka, 2006; U.S. General Accountability Office, 2003). Many other examples exist in the United States and elsewhere.

There are many considerations involved in selecting and implementing new crime prevention programs (as well as in expanding effective programs or putting an end to ineffective or harmful ones). For example, there may be different government priorities, such as military defense spending, environmental protection, or prescription drug benefits for seniors, which are competing for scarce public resources. National polls may show that the public is more concerned with policy issues other than crime prevention. Other political considerations include the worry by politicians that they may be perceived as soft on crime by supporting non–criminal justice crime prevention efforts (see Gest, 2001), as well as the short time horizons of politicians (Tonry and Farrington, 1995b), which makes programs that show results only in the longer term less appealing to those who come up for election every few years. Regrettably, it seems that evidence of what works best is rarely a factor in choosing which new programs should be implemented. Political considerations and media headlines seem to dominate.

Evidence-based crime prevention attempts to avoid these mistakes by ensuring that the best available evidence is considered in any decision to implement a program designed to prevent crime. As noted by Anthony Petrosino (2000, p. 635), "An evidence-based approach requires that the results of rigorous evaluation be rationally integrated into decisions about interventions by policymakers and practitioners alike."

The evidence-based approach has garnered much support in medicine (Halladay and Bero, 2000; Millenson, 1997). Even in medicine, a discipline noted for its adherence to scientific principles and high educational requirements, most practice is "shaped by local custom, opinions, theories, and subjective impressions" (Sherman, 1998, p. 6). Of course, making available scientific evidence on what works best to policy makers and practitioners (regardless of the discipline) and having them put it into practice are two entirely different things.

The Evidence-Based Model

In characterizing the evidence-based model and its application to crime prevention, it is important to first define what is meant by the word *evidence*. *Evidence* is taken to mean scientific, not criminal evidence (see Sherman, 1998, p. 2, n. 1). Evidence introduced in criminal court proceedings, though bound by laws and procedures, is altogether different from scientific evidence. The latter "refers to its common usage in science to distinguish data from theory, where evidence is defined as 'facts ... in support of a conclusion, statement or belief'" (*Shorter Oxford English Dictionary*, 2002, as cited in Sherman, 2003, p. 7).

Politics, Theory, and Method

Although it is acknowledged that evidence-based crime prevention can serve other useful purposes—for example, improving police training standards, improving community relations, and so on—the main outcome of interest or bottom line is crime prevention. The parallel is with evidence-based medicine's primary focus on saving lives or improving the quality of life for those suffering from terminal or chronic illnesses. For evidence-based crime prevention, the prevention of crime is a first-tier or primary outcome.

At the heart of the evidence-based model is the notion that "we are all entitled to our own opinions, but not to our own facts" (Sherman, 1998, p. 4). Use of opinions instead of facts to guide crime policy may cause harmful or iatrogenic effects (McCord, 2003), lead to the implementation of programs that do not work at all, waste scarce public resources (Welsh and Farrington, 2000), and divert policy attention from the most pressing crime prevention priorities of the day. Moreover, within the evidence-based paradigm, drawing conclusions based on facts calls attention to two fundamental issues: (1) the validity of the evidence, and (2) the methods used to locate, appraise, and synthesize the evidence. (These are described in detail here.)

Part of a Larger Movement

Evidence-based crime prevention is a part of a larger and increasingly expanding evidence-based movement. In general terms, this movement is dedicated to the betterment of society through the utilization of the highest quality scientific evidence on what works best. The evidence-based movement first began in medicine (Millenson, 1997) and has more recently been embraced by the social sciences (Mosteller and Boruch, 2002; Sherman, 2003; Sherman, Farrington, Welsh, and MacKenzie, 2006; Welsh and Farrington, 2006c).

In 1993, the Cochrane Collaboration was established to prepare, maintain, and make accessible systematic reviews of research on the effects of health care and medical interventions. The Cochrane Collaboration established collaborative review groups (CRGs) across the world to oversee the preparation and maintenance of systematic reviews in specific areas, such as coronary heart disease and cancer treatment. All reviews produced by Cochrane CRGs follow a uniform structure. The same level of detail and consistency of reporting is found in each, and each review is made accessible through the *Cochrane Library*, a quarterly electronic publication. In the

United Kingdom, the National Institute for Clinical Excellence depends heavily on Cochrane reviews in deciding whether a treatment can be provided as part of the National Health Service.

The success of the Cochrane Collaboration in reviewing the effectiveness of medical and health care interventions stimulated international interest in establishing a similar infrastructure for research on the effects of interventions in the social sciences, including education, social work and social welfare, and crime and justice. In 2000, the Campbell Collaboration was established. It is named after the influential experimental psychologist Donald T. Campbell (see Campbell, 1969). The collaboration's Crime and Justice Group aims to prepare and maintain systematic reviews of criminological interventions and make them accessible electronically to practitioners, policy makers, scholars, and the general public (Farrington and Petrosino, 2001).

Evaluation Research

When can we have confidence that the reported conclusions of an evaluation of a crime prevention program—whether they suggest that it is effective, ineffective, or, worse yet, harmful—are valid? This is a central question for an evidence-based approach to preventing crime.

High-Quality Evaluations

It is surely stating the obvious to say that not all evaluations of crime prevention programs are equally valid. The methodological quality of evaluations can vary greatly. According to Donald Campbell and his colleagues (Campbell and Stanley, 1966; Cook and Campbell, 1979; Shadish, Cook, and Campbell, 2002), the methodological quality of evaluation studies depends on four criteria: statistical conclusion validity, internal validity, construct validity, and external validity.[1] "Validity refers to the correctness of inferences about cause and effect" (Shadish et al., 2002, p. 34).

Statistical conclusion validity is concerned with whether the presumed cause (the intervention) and the presumed effect (the outcome) are related. The main threats to this form of validity are insufficient statistical power[2] to detect the effect (e.g., because of small sample size) and the use of inappropriate statistical techniques.

Internal validity refers to how well the study unambiguously demonstrates that an intervention (e.g., closed-circuit television or CCTV) had an effect on an outcome (e.g., crime). In this case, some kind of control condition is necessary to estimate what would have happened to the experimental units (e.g., people or areas) if the intervention had not been applied to them—called the "counterfactual inference." The main threats to internal validity are as follows (Shadish et al., 2002, p. 55).

- Selection: The effect reflects preexisting differences between experimental and control conditions.
- History: The effect is caused by some event occurring at the same time as the intervention.
- Maturation: The effect reflects a continuation of preexisting trends, for example, in normal human development or in crime rates.
- Instrumentation: The effect is caused by a change in the method of measuring the outcome.
- Testing: The pretest measurement causes a change in the posttest measure.
- Regression to the mean: Where an intervention is implemented on units with unusually high scores (e.g., areas with high crime rates), natural fluctuation will cause a decrease in these scores on the posttest, which might be mistakenly interpreted as an effect of the intervention. The opposite (an increase) can happen when the interventions are applied to low-crime areas or low-scoring people.[3]
- Differential attrition: The effect is caused by differential loss of units (e.g., people) from experimental compared to control conditions.
- Causal order: It is unclear whether the intervention preceded or followed the effect (e.g., a change in crime rates).

Construct validity refers to the adequacy of the operational definition and measurement of the theoretical constructs that underlie the intervention and the outcome. For example, if a CCTV project aims to investigate the effect of increased surveillance on offending, did CCTV really cause an increase in surveillance? The main threats to this form of validity rest on the extent to which the intervention succeeded in changing what it was intended to change (e.g., to what extent was there treatment fidelity or implementation failure) and on the validity and reliability of outcome measures (e.g., how adequately police-recorded crime rates reflect true crime rates).

External validity refers to how well the effect of an intervention on an outcome is generalizable or replicable in different conditions: different operational definitions of the intervention and various outcomes, different persons, different environments, and so on. It is difficult to investigate this within one evaluation study. External validity can be established more convincingly in systematic reviews and meta-analyses of a number of evaluation studies (see following discussion). As noted by William Shadish and colleagues (2002, p. 87), the main threats to this form of validity consist of interactions of causal relationships (effect sizes) with types of persons, settings, interventions, and outcomes. For example, an intervention designed to reduce crime may be effective with some types of people and in some kinds of places but not in other cases. A key issue is whether the effect size varies according to the degree to which those who carried out the research had some kind of stake in the results. Independent evaluations are best.

An evaluation of a crime prevention program is considered to be of high quality if it possesses a high degree of internal, construct, and statistical conclusion validity. Put another way, we can have a great deal of confidence in the observed effects of an intervention if it has been evaluated using a design that controls for the major threats to these three forms of validity. Experimental (randomized and nonrandomized) and quasi-experimental research designs are the types that can best achieve this aim.

Most evaluations of situational crime prevention programs are called area-based studies. In these studies, the effect of crime on the area or place (e.g., neighborhood, school, public housing community) is measured, rather than the effect of crime on the individual, which is assessed in commonly used evaluation studies. In area-based studies, the best and most feasible design usually involves before-and-after measures of crime in experimental and comparable control conditions, together with statistical control of extraneous variables. This is an example of a quasi-experimental evaluation design. All of the evaluations of the different forms of surveillance measures reviewed in this book used this type of design.

We would have preferred that the evaluations employed a randomized experimental design. This is because the randomized experiment is the most convincing method of evaluating crime prevention programs (Farrington, 1983; Farrington and Welsh, 2005, 2006a).[4] However, unlike in medicine, psychology, and other social science fields like education, there are few randomized experiments in criminology (Sherman, 2003). Even fewer area-based studies employ such designs (Weisburd, 2005). Random assignment is problematic in the design of area-based studies. The difficulty stems primarily from the need to randomize a large enough number of areas to gain the benefits of randomization in equating experimental and control areas on all possible extraneous variables (within the limits of statistical fluctuation). As a rule of thumb, at least 50 units in each category are needed (Farrington, 1997). This number is relatively easy to achieve with individuals but very difficult to achieve with larger units, such as communities, schools, classrooms, or areas. There have been some experiments (e.g., on hot spots policing—see Farrington and Welsh, 2005, 2006a) in which 100 or more areas were randomly assigned to conditions, but no experiment of this kind has yet been conducted to investigate the effectiveness of surveillance techniques such as CCTV and improved lighting. Another important limiting factor is the cost associated with the area-based evaluation design.

In our reviews, we have ensured that only the most rigorous quasi-experimental evaluations are considered. We required not only control conditions but also prior measures of crime in both experimental and control conditions, so that changes in crime rates could be assessed in both conditions. In some cases, we contacted the authors of studies to obtain key information, for example, to verify the comparability of the experimental and control areas. With these and other efforts, we are confident that we have brought together the best available research evidence to assess the effectiveness of the major forms of surveillance to prevent crime in public places.

Assessing Research Evidence

Just as it is crucial to use the highest quality evaluation designs to investigate the effects of crime prevention programs, it is also important to use the most rigorous methods to assess the available research evidence. Efforts to assess if a particular prevention strategy (e.g., situational, community), intervention modality (e.g., CCTV, improved lighting), or some other grouping of prevention programs is effective in preventing crime can take many different forms. The systematic review and the meta-analytic review (or meta-analysis) are the most rigorous methods for assessing effectiveness (Welsh and Farrington, 2001, 2006a).[5] These are the sources we rely on most in our reviews of the effectiveness of the different types of surveillance programs designed to prevent crime in chapters 5–7.

Systematic Reviews

According to Byron Johnson and his colleagues (2000, p. 35), systematic reviews "essentially take an epidemiological look at the methodology and results sections of a specific population of studies to reach a research-based consensus on a given study topic." Such reviews use rigorous methods for locating, appraising, and synthesizing evidence from prior evaluation studies, and they are reported with the same level of detail that characterizes high-quality reports of original research. Some of the key features of a systematic review include the following.

- The eligibility criteria are explicit. The reviewers specify in detail why they included certain studies and rejected others. What was the minimum level of methodological quality? Did they consider only a particular type of evaluation design, such as randomized experiments?[6] What types of interventions were included? What kinds of outcome data had to be reported in the studies? In the final report, the reviewers should explicitly present all the criteria or rules used in selecting eligible studies.
- The search for studies is designed to reduce potential bias. Because there are many possible ways that bias can compromise the results of a review, reviewers must explicitly state how they conducted their search of potentially relevant studies to reduce such bias. How did they try to locate studies reported outside scientific journals? How did they try to locate studies reported in foreign languages? All bibliographic databases that were searched should be made explicit so that potential gaps in coverage can be identified.
- Each study is screened according to eligibility criteria, with exclusions justified. The searches will undoubtedly locate many citations and abstracts to potentially relevant studies. Each

report of these potentially relevant studies must be screened to determine whether the study meets the eligibility criteria for the review. A full listing of excluded studies and the justifications for exclusion should be made available to readers.

- The most complete data possible are assembled. The systematic reviewer will generally try to obtain all relevant evaluations meeting the eligibility criteria. In addition, all data relevant to the objectives of the review should be carefully extracted from each eligible report, coded, and computerized. Sometimes, original study documents lack important information. When possible, the systematic reviewer attempts to obtain these data from the authors of the original reports.
- Quantitative techniques are used, when appropriate and possible, in analyzing results. A systematic review may or may not include a meta-analysis (see appendix). The use of meta-analysis may not be appropriate because of a small number of studies, heterogeneity across studies, or different units of analysis of the studies (i.e., a mix of area- and individual-based studies). When suitable, meta-analyses should be conducted as part of systematic reviews.
- The report is structured and detailed. The final report of a systematic review is structured and detailed so that the reader can understand each phase of the research, the decisions made, and the conclusions reached.

As noted by Anthony Petrosino and colleagues (2001, p. 20), "the foremost advantage of systematic reviews is that when done well and with full integrity, they provide the most reliable and comprehensive statement about what works." They are not, however, without their limitations, although these limitations or challenges appear to be most closely linked with administrative and dissemination issues, such as getting them in the hands of decision makers (see Petrosino, Boruch, Soydan, Duggan, and Sanchez-Meca, 2001). Some of the challenges involving the "substance" of systematic reviews include the transparency of the process (e.g., the need to present the reasons that studies were included or excluded) and the need to reconcile differences in coding of study characteristics and outcomes by multiple researchers (e.g., by measuring interrater reliability).

Meta-Analytic Reviews

A meta-analysis addresses the question: How well does the program work? It involves the statistical or quantitative analysis of the results of prior research studies (Lipsey and Wilson, 2001). Because it involves the statistical summary of data (in particular, effect sizes), it requires a reasonable number of intervention studies that are sufficiently similar to be grouped together; there may be little point in reporting an average effect size based on a small number of studies. Nevertheless, quantitative methods can be very important in helping a reviewer determine the average effect of a particular intervention.

One major product of a meta-analysis is a weighted average effect size. For example, the percentage reduction in offending would be one simple effect size. In calculating the average, each effect size is usually weighted according to the sample size on which it is based, with larger studies having greater weights. There is usually an attempt to investigate factors (moderators) that predict larger or smaller effect sizes in different studies. This is done to establish whether an intervention works better in certain contexts and which features of the intervention are most related to a successful outcome.

Some of the strengths of the meta-analytic review method include its transparent nature—the explication of its methods and the studies involved—which makes it easily replicated by other researchers and its ability to handle a large number of studies that may be overwhelming for other review methods. In addition, the "statistical methods of meta-analysis help guard against interpreting the dispersion in results as meaningful when it can just as easily be explained as sampling error" (Wilson, 2001, p. 84). Limitations of meta-analysis include, on a practical side, its time-consuming nature and its inability to synthesize "complex patterns of effects found in individual studies" (Wilson, 2001, p. 84). Another problem concerns how to select effect sizes for analysis in studies that report many different outcomes.

Assessing Value for Money

Assessing the value for money of crime prevention programs is closely linked to evidence-based crime prevention. A fair and reliable assessment of a program's value for money is the purview of economic analysis. An economic analysis (e.g., cost-benefit analysis, cost-effectiveness analysis; see following discussion for details) can be described as a policy tool that allows choices to be made between alternative uses of resources or alternative distributions of services (Knapp, 1997, p. 11). Many criteria are used in economic analysis. The most common is efficiency, or value for money (achieving maximum outcomes from minimum inputs). However, the specific focus on economic efficiency is not meant to imply that crime prevention programs should be continued only if their benefits outweigh their costs. There are many important noneconomic criteria on which these programs should be judged (e.g., equity in the distribution of services).

We report monetary costs and benefits (where available) in our reviews of the effectiveness of the different types of surveillance programs in the next three chapters. Of the two main techniques of economic analysis—cost-benefit and cost-effectiveness analysis—only cost-benefit analysis allows for an assessment of both costs and benefits. A cost-effectiveness analysis can be referred to as an incomplete cost-benefit analysis. This is because no attempt is made to estimate the monetary value of program effects (benefits or disbenefits), only resources used (costs). For example, a cost-effectiveness analysis might specify how many crimes were prevented per $1,000 spent on a program. Another way to think about how cost-benefit and cost-effectiveness analysis differ is that "cost-effectiveness analysis may help one decide among competing program models, but it cannot show that the total effect was worth the cost of the program" (Weinrott, Jones, and Howard, 1982, p. 179), unlike cost-benefit analysis.

A cost-benefit analysis is a step-by-step process that follows a standard set of procedures. There are six main steps: (1) define the scope of the analysis; (2) obtain estimates of program effects; (3) estimate the monetary value of costs and benefits; (4) calculate present value and assess profitability; (5) describe the distribution of costs and benefits (an assessment of who gains and who loses, e.g., program participant, government/taxpayer, crime victim); and (6) conduct sensitivity analyses by varying the different assumptions made (Barnett, 1993, pp. 143–148).[7]

A major aim in a cost-benefit analysis is to produce a benefit-to-cost ratio for an intervention. For example, Lawrence Schweinhart, Helen Barnes, and David Weikart (1993) estimated that for every child who received the Perry preschool program, $7 were saved for every $1 expended on the program (mainly because the program reduced the arrest rate by half). This kind of information often has a big influence on practitioners and policy makers and can be crucial in encouraging them to implement programs.

Two other key features of economic analysis require brief mention. First, an economic analysis is an extension of an outcome or impact evaluation, and it is only as defensible as the evaluation on which it is based. David Weimer and Lee Friedman (1979, p. 264) recommended that economic analyses be limited to programs that have been evaluated with an "experimental or strong quasi-experimental design." As mentioned, the most convincing method of evaluating crime prevention programs is to conduct a randomized experiment.

Second, many perspectives can be taken in measuring program costs and benefits. Some cost-benefit analyses adopt a society-wide perspective that includes the major parties who can receive benefits or incur costs, such as the government or taxpayer, crime victim, and program participant. Other analyses may take a more narrow view, focusing on only one or two of these parties. The decision about which perspective to take has important implications for evaluating a program, particularly if it is being funded by public money. That is, if conclusions are to be drawn about the monetary benefits or costs of a program to the public, the benefits or costs must be those that the public will either receive or incur. In reporting on the cost-benefit findings of the studies we review in the next three chapters, we have used, as far as possible, a middle-of-the-road approach—focusing on the costs and benefits for the government or taxpayer and for crime victims.

Displacement and Diffusion Effects

Also important in our reviews of the effectiveness of the major forms of surveillance that are used to prevent crime are the issues of displacement of crime and diffusion of crime prevention benefits.

Displacement, often considered the Achilles heel of situational crime prevention, can be defined as the unintended increase in crimes following the introduction of a crime reduction scheme. (For a discussion of benign or desirable effects of displacement, see Barr and Pease, 1990.) This is the notion that offenders simply move around the corner or resort to different methods to commit crimes once a prevention project has been introduced. More than 30 years ago, Thomas Reppetto (1976) identified five different forms of displacement: temporal (change in time), tactical (change in method), target (change in victim), territorial (change in place), and functional (change in type of crime).

Diffusion of benefits, on the other hand, can be defined as the unintended decrease in nontargeted crimes following from a crime reduction scheme, or the "complete reverse" of displacement (Clarke and Weisburd, 1994). Here, instead of a prevention project displacing crime, the project's benefits are diffused to the surrounding area, for example. Ronald Clarke and David Weisburd (1994) contend that diffusion occurs in one of two ways: by affecting offenders' assessment of risk (deterrence) or by affecting offenders' assessment of effort and reward (discouragement).[8]

To investigate these topics, the minimum design should involve one experimental area, one adjacent area, and one nonadjacent comparable control area. If crime decreased in the experimental area, increased in the adjacent area, and stayed constant in the control area, this might be evidence of displacement. If crime decreased in the experimental and adjacent areas and stayed constant or increased in the control area, this might be evidence of diffusion of benefits.

Conclusions

An evidence-based approach is crucial to understanding where, when, and whether different interventions prevent crime, as well as helping establish why an intervention did or did not work. Crime policy is rarely formulated on the basis of hard evidence, but support for evidence-based crime prevention is growing. This growth has been fostered by a number of recent developments, including a movement toward an evidence-based approach in other disciplines, such as medicine (Millenson, 1997) and education (Mosteller and Boruch, 2002); large-scale, government- and foundation-sponsored reviews of "what works" in crime prevention (Goldblatt and Lewis, 1998; Sherman et al., 1997; 2006; Tonry and Farrington, 1995a); and, most recently, the establishment of the Campbell Collaboration and its Crime and Justice Group (Welsh and Farrington, 2006a).

In the next three chapters, we review the empirical evidence on the effectiveness of surveillance for crime prevention in public space.

Part II

Evidence of Effectiveness

Closed-Circuit Television

5

Closed-circuit television (CCTV) surveillance cameras serve many functions and are used in both public and private settings. One of their primary objectives in public places is to prevent personal and property crime. CCTV is also used to aid police in the detection and apprehension of suspects, aid in the prosecution of alleged offenders, improve police officer safety and compliance with the law (through, for instance, cameras mounted on the dashboard of police cruisers to record police stops, searches, and so on), and assist in the detection and prevention of terrorist activities. The focus here is on the effectiveness of CCTV in preventing crime. This is because few evaluations (and, to our knowledge, no high-quality ones) have assessed the impact of these other uses of public CCTV.

This chapter reviews the scientific evidence on the effectiveness of CCTV to prevent crime in public places. It reports on the results of a new update of our systematic review (Welsh and Farrington, 2002, 2004a, 2004b, 2006b).

Results

Evaluations were included in the systematic review if they met a number of criteria, including if CCTV was the main intervention, if there was an outcome measure of crime, and if the evaluation design was of high methodological quality. (See appendix for full details on the methodology of the systematic review and meta-analysis.) A number of search strategies were used to locate studies meeting the criteria for inclusion, including searches of electronic bibliographic databases, searches of literature reviews on the effectiveness of CCTV on crime, and contacts with leading researchers. Altogether, 44 studies met our inclusion criteria, and 41 of these could be used in the meta-analysis.[1]

In addition to conducting a meta-analysis, each included evaluation was rated on its effectiveness in reducing crime. Each evaluation was assigned to one of the following four categories: desirable effect (marked decrease in crime), undesirable effect (marked increase in crime), null effect (evidence of no effect on crime), or uncertain effect (unclear evidence of an effect on crime). (The same rating scale is used in chapters 6 and 7.)

Setting

Forty-one of the 44 CCTV evaluations were carried out in four main settings: city and town centers, public housing, public transport, and car parks. The remaining three evaluations were carried out in residential areas (n = 2) and a hospital.

City and Town Centers

Twenty-two evaluations met the criteria for inclusion and were carried out in city and town centers. Seventeen of these were carried out in the United Kingdom, 3 in the United States, 1 in Sweden, and 1 in Norway (see table 5.1). Only some of the studies reported the coverage of the CCTV cameras. For example, in the Newcastle-upon-Tyne and Malmö studies, camera coverage of the target or experimental area was 100%. Many more studies reported the number of cameras used and their features (e.g., pan, tilt, zoom). Information on camera coverage is important because if a large enough section of the target area or even high-crime locations in the target area are not under surveillance, the impact of CCTV may be reduced.

Most of the evaluations that reported information on the monitoring of the cameras used active monitoring, meaning that an operator watched monitors linked to the cameras in real time. Passive monitoring involves watching recordings of camera footage at a later time. In some of the schemes, such as in Newcastle and Birmingham, police carried out active monitoring. More often it was carried out by security personnel who had some form of communication link with police (e.g., by a one-way radio, direct-line telephone).

On average, the follow-up period in the 22 evaluations was 15 months, ranging from a low of 3 months to a high of 60 months. Six programs included other interventions in addition to the main intervention of CCTV. For example, in the Doncaster program, 47 help-points were established within the target area to aid the public in contacting the main CCTV control room. Four other studies used notices of CCTV to inform the public that they were under surveillance, but these notices do not necessarily constitute a secondary intervention. A couple of the evaluations used multiple experimental areas (e.g., police beats), meaning that the CCTV intervention was quite extensive in the city or town center. Multiple control areas (e.g., adjacent police beats, the remainder of the city) were used in many more of the evaluations. Where control and adjacent areas were used, we analyzed control areas.

As shown in table 5.1, the city and town center CCTV evaluations showed mixed results in their effectiveness in reducing crime. Ten of the 22 evaluations were considered to have a desirable effect on crime, 5 were considered to have an undesirable effect, and 1, the multisite British evaluation by Sivarajasingam, Shepherd, and Matthews (2003), was considered to have both (desirable effects according to emergency department admissions and undesirable effects according to police records). The remaining six evaluations were considered to have a null (n = 5) or uncertain (n = 1) effect on crime. Schemes usually showed evidence of no displacement rather than displacement or diffusion of benefits.

In the program evaluated by Rachel Armitage, Graham Smyth, and Ken Pease (1999), an unknown number of cameras were installed in the town center of Burnley, England. The experimental area consisted of police beats in the town center with CCTV coverage. Two control areas were used. The first comprised those police beats that shared a common boundary with the beats covered by CCTV. The second control area consisted of other police beats in the division. The first control area was more comparable to the experimental area. After 12 months, the experimental area, compared with the two control areas, showed substantial reductions in violent crime, burglary, vehicle crime, and total crime. For example,

Table 5.1
CCTV Evaluations in City and Town Centers

Author, Publication Date, Location	Camera Coverage and Monitoring	Other Interventions	Outcome Measure	Follow-up Period	Results and Diffusion/Displacement
Brown (1995), Newcastle-upon-Tyne, U.K.	Full coverage of most vulnerable premises on streets, active monitoring	None	Crime (total and types of offenses)	15 months	Undesirable effect; some displacement and diffusion
Brown (1995), Birmingham, U.K.	14 cameras, active monitoring by police	None	Crime (total and types of offenses)	12 months	Desirable effect; displacement occurred
Sarno (1996), London borough of Sutton, U.K.	11 cameras, n.a.	None	Crime (total and types of offenses)	12 months	Undesirable effect; not measured
Skinns (1998), Doncaster, U.K.	63 cameras, active monitoring by police	47 "help points" for public to contact CCTV control rooms	Crime (total and types of offenses)	24 months	Desirable effect; no displacement
Squires (1998), Ilford, U.K.	n.a., n.a.	None	Crime (total and types of offenses)	7 months	Desirable effect; displacement occurred
Armitage et al. (1999), Burnley, U.K.	n.a., n.a.	None	Crime (total and types of offenses)	12 months	Desirable effect; diffusion occurred
Ditton and Short (1999), Airdrie, U.K.	12 cameras, active monitoring by police	None	Crime (total and types of offenses)	24 months	Desirable effect; diffusion occurred
Sarno et al. (1999), London borough of Southwark (Elephant and Castle), U.K.	34 cameras, active monitoring	Notices of CCTV	Crime (total)	24 months	Null effect; possible evidence of diffusion

Study	Description	Signs	Outcome measure	Duration	Effect
Sarno et al. (1999), London borough of Southwark (Camberwell), U.K.	17 cameras, active monitoring sometimes by police	Notices of CCTV	Crime (total)	12 months	Desirable effect; no displacement
Sarno et al. (1999), London borough of Southwark (East Street), U.K.	12 cameras, active monitoring sometimes by police	Notices of CCTV	Crime (total)	12 months	Uncertain effect; no diffusion; possible functional displacement
Mazerolle et al. (2002), Cincinnati (Northside)	n.a., passive monitoring	None	Calls for service	6 months	Null effect; little or no displacement
Mazerolle et al. (2002), Cincinnati (Hopkins Park)	n.a., passive monitoring	None	Calls for service	4 months	Null effect; not measured
Mazerolle et al. (2002), Cincinnati (Findlay Market)	n.a., passive monitoring	None	Calls for service	3.5 months	Null effect; some displacement
Blixt (2003), Malmö (Möllevång Square), Sweden	100%, passive monitoring	Social improvement programs (begun years prior)	Violent crime (assault, serious assault, robbery)	12 months	Desirable effect; no displacement
Sivarajasingam et al. (2003), multiple city and town centers, U.K.	n.a., active monitoring by police and local council with links to police	None	Assault with injury (total) and violent crime (total)	24 months	Desirable effect (emergency department), undesirable effect (police); not measured

(*Continued*)

Table 5.1 (*continued*)

Author, Publication Date, Location	Camera Coverage and Monitoring	Other Interventions	Outcome Measure	Follow-up Period	Results and Diffusion/ Displacement
Winge and Knutsson (2003), Oslo, Norway	6 cameras, active monitoring with links to police	Notices of CCTV	Crime (total and types of offenses)	12 months	Undesirable effect; no displacement
Gill and Spriggs (2005), Borough Town, U.K.	70%, active monitoring with one-way link to police	None	Crime (total and types of offenses)	12 months	Desirable effect; no displacement
Gill and Spriggs (2005), Market Town, U.K.	34%, active monitoring with direct line to police	Community wardens, car park	Crime (total and types of offenses)	12 months	Undesirable effect; no displacement
Gill and Spriggs (2005), Shire Town, U.K.	76%, active monitoring	Community wardens	Crime (total and types of offenses)	12 months	Desirable effect; no displacement
Gill and Spriggs (2005), South City, U.K.	72%, active monitoring with police in room	Community wardens, police operations	Crime (total and types of offenses)	12 months	Null effect; no displacement
Farrington et al. (2007), Cambridge, U.K.	30 cameras, n.a.	None	Crime (total and types of offenses)	11 months	Undesirable effect; not measured
Griffiths (no date), Gillingham, U.K.	n.a., active monitoring	Improved lighting, neighborhood watch, "shop safe" network (radio link for shops to report crime)	Crime (total and types of offenses)	60 months	Desirable effect; not measured

Notes: n.a. = not available. The location names for the four evaluations by Gill and Spriggs (2005) are pseudonyms.

total incidents of crime fell by 28% in the experimental area, compared with a slight decline of 1% in the first control area and an increase of 10% in the second control area. The authors found evidence of diffusion of benefits for the categories of total crime, violent crime, and vehicle crime and evidence of territorial displacement for burglary.

In the program evaluated by University of Glamorgan criminologist Trevor Bennett and us (Farrington, Bennett, and Welsh, 2007), 30 cameras were installed in the city center of Cambridge, England. The control area was a secondary city center shopping area where there were no cameras on the streets. Comparing 11 months after the cameras were installed with the same 11-month period of the year before, police-recorded crimes had decreased by 14% in the experimental area and by 27% in the control area. Hence, there was an undesirable effect of CCTV on police-recorded crimes. Violent crimes (assault and robbery) also decreased more in the control area, and vehicle crimes (theft of and from vehicles) decreased equally in the experimental and control areas. Interviews were also carried out with quota samples of persons in the areas before and after the CCTV installation, asking them about their victimization (insulted or bothered, threatened, assaulted, or mugged) in the previous 12 months. The percentage victimized increased from 26% to 29% in the experimental area and from 11% to 14% in the control area, suggesting that the installation of CCTV had no effect on victimization. These results suggested that CCTV may have had no effect on crime but may have caused increased reporting to and/or recording by the police.

In pooling the data from the 20 studies for which effect sizes could be calculated, there was evidence that CCTV led to a small but nonsignificant reduction in crime in city and town centers. The weighted mean effect size was an odds ratio of 1.08, which corresponds to a 7% reduction in crimes in experimental areas compared with control areas. However, when these 20 studies were disaggregated by country, the 15 British studies showed a slightly larger effect on crime (a 10% decrease), whereas the 5 others showed no effect on crime.

Public Housing

Nine evaluations were carried out in public housing. Seven were carried out in the United Kingdom and two in the United States (see table 5.2). Camera coverage ranged from a low of 9% (in Dual Estate) to a high of 87%

(in Northern Estate) in the six evaluations that reported this information. Active monitoring was used in all of the schemes, with monitoring in the Brooklyn evaluation conducted by police. In the six British schemes evaluated by Martin Gill and Angela Spriggs (2005), security personnel who monitored the cameras had some form of communication link with police (i.e., a one-way or two-way radio). On average, the follow-up period in the nine evaluations was 12 months, ranging from a low of 3 months to a high of 18 months. Only three schemes included other interventions in addition to the main intervention of CCTV. These involved improved lighting and youth inclusion projects, which are community-run programs designed "to include socially excluded young people in mainstream society" through the provision of youth work, sport, and other activities (Bottoms and Dignan, 2004, p. 152).

As shown in table 5.2, the public housing CCTV evaluations showed mixed results in their effectiveness in reducing crime. Three of the nine evaluations were considered to have a desirable effect on crime, two had an undesirable effect, three had an uncertain effect, and one had a null effect. Only five schemes measured diffusion or displacement, and in each case it was reported that displacement did not occur.

In pooling the data from the eight studies for which effect sizes could be calculated, there was evidence that CCTV led to a small but nonsignificant reduction in crime in public housing. The weighted mean effect size was an odds ratio of 1.07, which corresponds to a 7% reduction in crimes in experimental areas compared with control areas.

The evaluation by Douglas Williamson and Sara McLafferty (2000) in Brooklyn, New York, the only one that could not be included in the meta-analysis, is somewhat representative of CCTV's rather negligible effect on crime in public housing. The housing community that received the intervention (Albany project) did not show any change in the total number of police-recorded crimes, either inside the project or inside a 0.1-mile buffer zone (established to measure displacement or diffusion), while total crime in the control community (Roosevelt project) dropped by 5% inside the project and 4% inside the 0.1-mile buffer zone. When total crime was disaggregated, a desirable program effect was observed for major felonies in both experimental and control projects. However, the authors note that "the substantial decrease in major felonies around both public housing projects seems to be part of a larger downward trend that was occurring not only in Brooklyn but across New York City in the late

Table 5.2
CCTV Evaluations in Public Housing

Author, Publication Date, Location	Camera Coverage and Monitoring	Other Interventions	Outcome Measure	Follow-up Period	Results and Diffusion/ Displacement
Musheno et al. (1978), Bronxdale Houses, New York City	Cameras in lobby and elevators; monitors in apartments	None	Crime (total and types offenses)	3 months	Uncertain effect; not measured
Williamson and McLafferty (2000), Brooklyn, New York	105 cameras, active monitoring by police	None	Crime (total and types of offenses)	18 months	Null effect; displacement and diffusion did not occur
Hood (2003), Greater Easterhouse Housing Estate, Glasgow, U.K.	n.a., active monitoring	None	Violent and drug crimes	20 months	Desirable effect; not measured
Gill and Spriggs (2005), Deploy Estate, U.K.	34%, active monitoring with one-way link to police	None	Crime (total and types of offenses)	12 months	Undesirable effect; no displacement
Gill and Spriggs (2005), Dual Estate, U.K.	9%, active monitoring with two-way link to police	None	Crime (total and types of offenses)	12 months	Uncertain effect; no displacement
Gill and Spriggs (2005), Southcap Estate, U.K.	73%, active monitoring with one-way link to police	Youth inclusion project	Crime (total and types of offenses)	6 months	Undesirable effect; not measured
Gill and Spriggs (2005), Eastcap Estate, U.K.	29%, active monitoring with two-way link to police	Improved lighting	Crime (total and types of offenses)	12 months	Uncertain effect; no displacement
Gill and Spriggs (2005), Northern Estate, U.K.	87%, active monitoring with one-way link to police	None	Crime (total and types of offenses)	12 months	Desirable effect; no displacement
Gill and Spriggs (2005), Westcap Estate, U.K.	62%, active monitoring	Youth inclusion project	Crime (total and types of offenses)	12 months	Desirable effect; not measured

Notes: n.a. = not available. The location names for the six evaluations by Gill and Spriggs (2005) are pseudonyms.

1990s" (Williamson and McLafferty, 2000, p. 7). Furthermore, the authors' investigation of the occurrence of displacement or diffusion of benefits concluded that there was "no clear evidence" of either, "as the change in crime around the two housing projects does not vary predictably with distance" (p. 7).

Public Transport

Four evaluations were carried out in public transportation systems. All of them were conducted in underground railway systems: three in the London Underground and one in the Montreal Metro (see table 5.3). None of the studies reported on the percentage of the target areas covered by the cameras, but most provided information on the number of cameras used. For example, in the Montreal program, a total of 130 cameras (approximately 10 per station) were installed in the experimental stations. Each of the schemes involved active monitoring on the part of police; in the London Underground, this meant the British Transport Police.

With the exception of the Montreal program, each evaluation included other interventions in addition to CCTV. In the first Underground scheme, special police patrols were in operation prior to the installation of CCTV.[2] For the two other Underground schemes, some of the other interventions included passenger alarms, kiosks to monitor CCTV, and mirrors. For each of these Underground schemes, CCTV was, however, the main intervention. The follow-up periods ranged from a low of 12 months to a high of 32 months.

Overall, CCTV programs in public transportation systems present conflicting evidence of effectiveness: two had a desirable effect, one had no effect, and one had an undesirable effect on crime. However, for the two effective programs in the London Underground (southern sector and Northern Line), the use of other interventions makes it difficult to say with certainty that it was CCTV that caused the observed crime reductions, although in the first of these programs CCTV was more than likely the cause (see note 2). In the second effective program, which included special police and Guardian Angels patrols, the words of the authors are instructive:

> It seems likely that robbery has been kept down by improved
> management and staffing of the system, including more revenue

Table 5.3

CCTV Evaluations in Public Transport

Author, Publication Date, Location	Camera Coverage and Monitoring	Other Interventions	Outcome Measure	Follow-up Period	Results and Diffusion/ Displacement
Burrows (1980), Underground subway (southern sector), London, U.K.	n.a., active monitoring by BTP	Notices of CCTV (special police patrols preceded CCTV)	Personal theft and robbery	12 months	Desirable effect; some displacement
Webb and Laycock (1992), Underground subway (Northern Line), London, U.K.	7–14 per E station, active monitoring by BTP	Passenger alarms, visible kiosk to monitor CCTV, mirrors, improved lighting	Robbery	26 months	Desirable effect; diffusion occurred
Webb and Laycock (1992), Underground subway (Oxford Circus station), London, U.K.	30 cameras, active monitoring by BTP	Passenger alarms, visible kiosk to monitor CCTV, BTP patrols	Personal theft, robbery, assault	32 months	Undesirable effect; not measured
Grandmaison and Tremblay (1997), Metro subway, Montreal, Canada	130 cameras (approx. 10 per E station), active monitoring by police	None	Crime (total and types of offenses)	18 months	Null effect; not measured

Notes: BTP = British Transport Police; E = experimental area; n.a. = not available.

protection as well as station staff. The policing changes may also have been helpful. It is also possible that the substantial physical work involved in station modernisation and the introduction of automatic ticket barriers in central area stations contributed by creating the impression of a more controlled and safer environment. (Webb and Laycock, 1992, p. 11)

Only two of the studies measured diffusion of benefits or displacement, with one showing evidence of diffusion and the other showing evidence of displacement.

In pooling the data from the four studies, there was evidence that CCTV led to a sizable but nonsignificant reduction in crime in public transport. The weighted mean effect size was an odds ratio of 1.30, which corresponds to a 23% reduction in crimes in experimental areas compared with control areas. The substantial reduction in robberies and thefts in the first Underground evaluation (an overall 61% decrease) was the main reason for this large average effect size over all four studies.

Car Parks or Parking Lots

Six CCTV evaluations met the criteria for inclusion and were conducted in car parks. All of the programs were implemented in the United Kingdom between the early 1980s and early 2000s (see table 5.4). Camera coverage was nearly 100% in the two schemes that reported on it. All of the studies, with the exception of one that did not provide data, involved active monitoring on the part of security staff. The large-scale, multisite Hawkeye scheme evaluated by Martin Gill and Angela Spriggs (2005) also included a radio link with the British Transport Police.

Each of the programs supplemented CCTV with other interventions, such as improved lighting, painting, fencing, payment schemes, and security personnel. In Coventry, for example, improved lighting, painting, and fencing were part of the package of measures implemented to reduce vehicle crimes. In each program, however, CCTV was the main intervention. The follow-up periods ranged from a low of 10 months to a high of 24 months.

Table 5.4 shows that five of the car park programs had a desirable effect and one had an undesirable effect on crime, with vehicle crimes being the exclusive focus of five of these evaluations. British criminologist Nick

Table 5.4
CCTV Evaluations in Parking Lots or Car Parks

Author, Publication Date, Location	Camera Coverage and Monitoring	Other Interventions	Outcome Measure	Follow-up Period	Results and Diffusion/ Displacement
Poyner (1991), University of Surrey, Guildford, U.K.	100% (almost), active monitoring	Improved lighting, foliage cut back	Theft of and from vehicles	10 months	Undesirable effect; diffusion occurred
Tilley (1993), Hartlepool, U.K.	n.a., active monitoring	Security officers, notices of CCTV, payment scheme	Theft of and from vehicles	30 months	Desirable effect; displacement occurred
Tilley (1993), Bradford, U.K.	n.a., active monitoring	Notices of CCTV, improved lighting, painting	Theft of and from vehicles	12 months	Desirable effect; not measured
Tilley (1993), Coventry, U.K.	n.a., active monitoring	Lighting, painting, fencing	Theft of and from vehicles	8 months (E) and 16 months (C)	Desirable effect; not measured
Sarno (1996), London borough of Sutton, U.K.	n.a., n.a.	Multiple (e.g., locking overnight, lighting)	Vehicle crime	12 months	Desirable effect; not measured
Gill and Spriggs (2005), multiple sites (Hawkeye), U.K.	95–100%, active monitoring with one-way link to BTP	Improved lighting, fencing, security	Crime (total)	12 months	Desirable effect; not measured

Notes: BTP = British Transport Police; E = experimental area; C = control area; n.a. = not available. Hawkeye is a pseudonym.

Tilley (1993) evaluated three CCTV programs in car parks in Hartlepool, Bradford, and Coventry. Each scheme was part of the British government's Safer Cities Programme, a large-scale crime prevention initiative that operated from the late 1980s to the mid-1990s. In Hartlepool, CCTV cameras were installed in a number of covered car parks, and the control area included a number of non–CCTV-covered car parks. Security personnel, notices of CCTV, and payment schemes were also part of the package of measures employed to reduce vehicle crimes. Twenty-four months after the program began, thefts of and from vehicles had been substantially reduced in the experimental compared with the control car parks. A 59% reduction in thefts of vehicles was observed in the experimental car parks, compared with a 16% reduction in the control car parks. Tilley (1993, p. 9) concluded that "The marked relative advantage of CCTV covered parks in relation to theft of cars clearly declines over time and there are signs that the underlying local trends [an increase in car thefts] begin to be resumed." The author suggested that the displacement of vehicle thefts from covered to noncovered car parks might have been partly responsible for this.

In the program evaluated by Christopher Sarno (1996), in the London borough of Sutton, CCTV cameras were installed in three car parks (the experimental area) in one part of the borough's police sector at high risk of vehicle crimes. Two control areas were established: the remainder of the borough's police sector and all of Sutton. The first control area was considered to be comparable to the experimental area.

The program was evaluated after its first 12 months of operation. Total vehicle crimes ("theft of, theft from, criminal damage to, unauthorised taking of vehicles and vehicle interference") were reduced by 57% in the experimental area, with slightly smaller reductions (36% and 40%) reported in the control areas where CCTV was not implemented. It is important to note that vehicle crimes were going down in the United Kingdom generally during this time period. Most studies, Sutton included, did not measure either diffusion of benefits or displacement.

The odds ratios showed a significant and desirable effect of CCTV for five of the schemes. In the other scheme (Guildford), the effect was undesirable, but the small number of crimes measured in the before and after periods meant that the odds ratio was not significant. When all six odds ratios were combined, the overall odds ratio was 2.03, meaning that crime decreased by half (51%) in experimental areas compared with control areas.

Other Settings

Three of the 44 included evaluations took place in other public settings: 2 in residential areas and 1 in a hospital. It was considered necessary to categorize these three schemes separately from the others because of the differences in the settings in which these programs were implemented as well as their small numbers. Table 5.5 provides information on the key characteristics of these CCTV evaluations (all of which took place in the United Kingdom) and their effects on crime.

There were some notable differences between the two residential schemes. The City Outskirts program was implemented in an economically depressed area on the outskirts of a Midlands city, whereas the Borough scheme was implemented throughout a southern borough of mixed

Table 5.5
CCTV Evaluations in Other Settings

Author, Publication Date, Location	Camera Coverage and Monitoring	Other Interventions	Outcome Measure	Follow-up Period	Results and Diffusion/ Displacement
Gill and Spriggs (2005), City Outskirts, U.K. (residential)	68%, active monitoring with direct line to police	Improved lighting, antiburglary schemes	Crime (total and types of offenses)	12 months	Desirable effect; no displacement
Gill and Spriggs (2005), Borough, U.K. (residential)	Low (8 re-deployable used), n.a.	None	Crime (total and types of offenses)	12 months	Undesirable effect; no displacement
Gill and Spriggs (2005), City Hospital, U.K. (hospital)	76%, active monitoring with direct line to police	Leaflets, posters, improved lighting, police operations	Crime (total and types of offenses)	12 months	Desirable effect; no displacement

Notes: n.a. = not available. The location names are pseudonyms.

affluence. Camera coverage was quite good in City Outskirts (68%), but not so in Borough. Martin Gill and Angela Spriggs (2005) noted that this was due in large measure to the use of redeployable cameras in Borough, whereas fixed cameras were used in City Outskirts. Other interventions were used in City Outskirts, but not in Borough. Evaluations of the schemes also found contrasting effects on crime: a significant desirable effect in City Outskirts (a 25% decrease) and a nearly significant undesirable effect in Borough (a 25% increase).

The one evaluation of CCTV implemented in a city hospital showed that it produced a desirable but nonsignificant effect on crime (odds ratio = 1.38), corresponding to a 28% decrease in crime in the experimental area compared with the control area. Among some of the scheme's distinguishing features, camera coverage was quite good (76%), active monitoring was used, there was a direct line between the camera operators and police, and other interventions were implemented, including improved lighting and police operations.

Crime Type

The major crime types that were reported were violence (including robbery) and vehicle crimes (including thefts of and from vehicles). Violence was reported in 23 evaluations, but CCTV had a desirable effect in reducing violence in only 3 cases (Airdrie, Malmö, and Shire Town). Overall, there was no effect of CCTV on violence (odds ratio = 1.03). Vehicle crimes were reported in 22 evaluations, and CCTV had a desirable effect in reducing them in 10 cases: in 5 of the 6 car park evaluations (all except Guildford), in 3 city or town center evaluations (Burnley, Gillingham, and South City), and in City Outskirts and City Hospital. Over all 22 evaluations, CCTV reduced vehicle crimes by 26% (odds ratio = 1.35). The greatest effect was in the large-scale, multisite Hawkeye study, but there was a significant effect even if this study was excluded (odds ratio = 1.28, corresponding to a 22% decrease in crimes).

Country Comparison

Of the 41 evaluations that were included in the meta-analysis, the overwhelming majority was carried out in the United Kingdom (n = 34). Five were from North America (four from the United States and one from

Canada), and the remaining two were from Sweden and Norway. When the pooled meta-analysis results were disaggregated by country, there was evidence that the use of CCTV to prevent crime was more effective in the United Kingdom than in other countries. In the British studies, CCTV had a significant desirable effect, with an overall 19% reduction in crime (odds ratio = 1.24). In the other studies, CCTV showed no desirable effect on crime (odds ratio = 0.97). Importantly, the significant results for the British studies were largely driven by the effective programs in car parks.

Pooled Effects

From the 41 evaluations that could be included in the meta-analysis, it was concluded that CCTV had a significant desirable effect on crime, with an overall 16% reduction in crime (odds ratio = 1.19). Figure 5.1 summarizes the results of the studies in a forest graph. It shows the odds ratio for total crime measured in each study plus its 95% confidence interval. The studies are ordered according to their magnitudes of their odds ratios. It can be seen that more than one-third (n = 15) showed evidence of a desirable effect of CCTV on crime, with odds ratios of 1.34 or greater (from City Outskirts upward, not including City Hospital). Fourteen of the 15 effective studies were carried out in the United Kingdom; the other was carried out in Sweden (Malmö). Three other studies showed a significant undesirable effect (Oslo, Cambridge, and Dual Estate), and the remaining 23 studies showed no significant effect.

Discussion and Conclusions

The studies included in this systematic review and meta-analysis showed that CCTV has a significant desirable effect on crime, is most effective in reducing crime in car parks, is most effective in reducing vehicle crimes, and has been more effective in reducing crime in the United Kingdom than in other countries.

The exact optimal circumstances for effective use of CCTV schemes are not entirely clear at present, and this needs to be established by future evaluation research. It is interesting to note that the success of the CCTV programs in car parks was mostly limited to a reduction in vehicle crimes (the only crime type measured in five of the six schemes) and camera

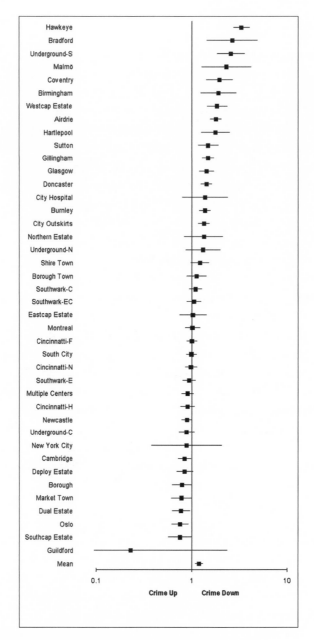

Figure 5.1 Meta-Analysis Results of CCTV Evaluations

Notes: Odds ratios on logarithmic scale; Southwark-EC = Elephant and Castle;
Southwark-C = Camberwell; Southwark-E = East Street; Cincinnati-N =
Northside; Cincinnati-H = Hopkins Park; Cincinnati-F = Findlay Market;
Multiple Centers = multiple city and town center study by Sivarajasingam,
Shepherd, and Matthews (2003); Underground-S = southern line;
Underground-N = northern line; Underground-C = Oxford Circus; Hawkeye =
multiple car parks study by Gill and Spriggs (2005).

coverage was high for those evaluations that reported on it. In the national British evaluation of the effectiveness of CCTV,[3] David Farrington, Martin Gill, Sam Waples, and Javier Argomaniz (2007) found that effectiveness was significantly correlated with the degree of coverage of the CCTV cameras, which was greatest in car parks. Furthermore, all six car park schemes included other interventions, such as improved lighting and security officers. It is plausible to suggest that CCTV schemes with high coverage and other interventions, targeted on vehicle crimes, are effective.

Conversely, the evaluations of CCTV schemes in city and town centers and public housing measured a much larger range of crime types, and only a few studies involved other interventions. These CCTV programs, as well as those focused on public transport, did not have a significant effect on crime.

Part of the difficulty in attempting to explain why CCTV schemes were more effective in reducing crime in car parks compared to other settings was that important information on implementation (e.g., How many cameras were installed and where? What was their degree of coverage of the targeted area? Were the cameras monitored? If so, for how long and by whom?) was not always reported in the evaluation studies. Of course, this lack of information is a problem in evaluations of other interventions as well.

Another dimension of this important issue concerns problems that occur following the implementation of CCTV cameras. This became a matter of some concern in Los Angeles's MacArthur Park—long considered a high-crime area—when it was discovered that a large number of the CCTV cameras were not working properly and some were not working altogether.[4] Reports of substantial reductions in gang activity and drug dealing followed the implementation of the cameras in March 2004. Serious crimes increased in the park in 2007, and the poorly functioning cameras were cited as one of the reasons for this increase. Other problems also plague the park's system of CCTV cameras. *Los Angeles Times* reporters Andrew Blankstein and Ari Bloomekatz (2008) note, "Problems extend beyond the ability of the cameras to pan the area. There have also been glitches with equipment that records and stores video images....In the case of the Rampart Division, data storage lasts only 12 hours before it is recorded over."

Another interesting finding to emerge from this review is that CCTV schemes in the United Kingdom showed a sizable (19%) and significant desirable effect on crime, whereas those in other countries showed no desirable effect on crime. (Even the Brooklyn public housing scheme that could not be included in the meta-analysis showed evidence of having no effect on crime. The Malmö, Sweden, city center scheme was the only effective one of those not included.) What might account for this? Or, more important, what lessons can be drawn from the British studies to help improve the crime prevention effectiveness of CCTV use in other countries, especially the United States? There were some differences in key characteristics between the British and other country CCTV programs, which may help address these questions.

First, the average follow-up period of the 8 other country CCTV schemes was substantially lower than for the 36 British schemes: 9.6 months versus 15.9–16.1 months. (Four of the other country studies had the shortest follow-up periods of all 44 CCTV evaluations, ranging from a low of 3 months to a high of 6 months.) Because of the short follow-up periods in the other country studies, it is possible that the programs were not given enough time to produce a clear effect on crime, either desirable or undesirable (six of the eight other country studies showed evidence of either a null or uncertain effect on crime). Longer follow-up periods, as in the majority of the British studies, seem to be warranted for future CCTV experiments in other countries, particularly in North America.

Second, and perhaps most important, not one of the 8 schemes from the other countries used other interventions alongside CCTV, whereas half of the 36 British schemes used one or more other types of intervention, such as improved lighting, fencing, security personnel, or youth inclusion projects. If the 6 car park schemes are removed (because all of them were carried out in the United Kingdom and involved other interventions), this leaves 12 out of 30 British studies that used other interventions. Possibly the absence of other situational or social crime prevention measures in the other country CCTV schemes may be a contributing factor to their overall poor effect in reducing crime; for example, CCTV on its own may not be seen as a sufficient deterrent threat to influence an offender's decision-making process to commit a crime or not.

Another important issue that may be a contributing factor to the difference in effectiveness between the British CCTV schemes and those in other countries is cultural context. In the United Kingdom, there is a high level of public support for the use of CCTV cameras in public settings to prevent crime (Norris and Armstrong, 1999; Norris and McCahill, 2006;

Phillips, 1999). In America (during the time that the few evaluations were conducted), the public was much less accepting and more apprehensive of CCTV's Big Brother implications (Murphy, 2002; Rosen, 2004). Furthermore, in the United States, resistance to the use of CCTV in public places (which continues to this day) also takes the form of legal action and constitutional challenges under the U.S. Constitution's Fourth Amendment prohibition against unreasonable searches and seizures (Nieto, 1997). In Sweden, Madeleine Blixt (2003) notes that surveillance cameras are highly regulated in public places, in almost all instances their use requiring a permit from the county administrative board. In Norway, Stig Winge and Johannes Knutsson (2003) note that there is a high degree of political scrutiny of public CCTV programs run by the police.

It could very well be that the overall poor showing of CCTV schemes in other countries was due in part to a lack of public support (and maybe even political support) for the schemes, which in turn may have resulted in reduced program funding, the police assigning lower priority to the schemes, or attempts to discourage desirable media coverage, for example. Each of these factors could potentially undermine the effectiveness of CCTV programs. In contrast, the British Home Office, which funded many of the U.K. evaluations, wanted to show that CCTV was effective because it had invested a lot of money in these schemes.

Disappointingly, little can be said about the monetary benefits of CCTV programs. Only 8 of the 44 programs conducted a cost-benefit analysis. In the Doncaster program, David Skinns (1998) found that the criminal justice costs saved from fewer prosecutions and sentences (the benefits) were greater than the costs of running the CCTV program by more than three times, for a benefit-to-cost ratio of 3.5 to 1. The other seven programs are part of the British national evaluation of CCTV conducted by Martin Gill and Angela Spriggs (2005). Cost-benefit analyses of these seven programs found mixed results: Three were worthwhile (the benefits from crimes prevented outweighed the costs of running the program), three were inefficient (the costs outweighed the benefits), and the multisite Hawkeye scheme was worthwhile in the highest risk car parks, with a benefit-to-cost ratio of 1.3 to 1, but not in the car parks judged to be low or medium risk. Gill and Spriggs found the cost-benefit results to be "unsurprising," largely owing to the programs having "little overall impact on the incidence of crime, but also because the systems' complexity made them expensive to set up and run" (2005, p. 114).

Unfortunately, these seven cost-benefit analyses were only carried out on those schemes where crime was reduced, however marginally, in the experimental area relative to the control area. This is less than adequate. Desirable results should not be the basis for deciding whether to conduct a cost-benefit or any other economic analysis; such analyses should be planned prospectively, not retrospectively.

Overall, it might be concluded that CCTV reduces crime in some circumstances. In light of the mixed results, future CCTV programs should be carefully implemented in different settings and should employ high-quality evaluation designs with long follow-up periods.

In the next chapter, we review and assess the effectiveness of improved street lighting to prevent crime in public places.

Improved Street Lighting

6

Improved street lighting serves many purposes, one of them being the prevention of crime in public places. Street lighting improvements are not always implemented with the express aim of preventing crime; pedestrian and traffic safety may be viewed as more important goals (see Beyer, Pond, and Ker, 2005). Although the notion of lighting streets to deter lurking criminals may be too simplistic, its relevance to the prevention of crime has been suggested in urban centers, residential areas, and other places frequented by potential criminals and potential victims (e.g., Clarke, 1995b; Jacobs, 1961).

The importance of street lighting to prevent crime became abundantly clear in Athens-Clarke County, Georgia, when commissioners voted to shut off about one-fifth (or 1,100) of the county's approximately 6,000 streetlights. No sooner had the decision been made public than residents began calling county commissioners and the city manager to complain about the plan. At the heart of the opposition was concern about property crime going up and increased fear of going out at night. Some of the commissioners also expressed concern that this action would lead to more crime, especially in the downtown neighborhoods. The commission's decision, taken in May 2008, was part of a larger effort to reduce the burden of a recent property tax increase. It was estimated that the reduction in streetlights would save taxpayers $109,500 each year (Aued, 2008a).

Within a few short months, however, county commissioners reversed their original decision to shut off the public streetlights, agreeing to only shut off those on private roads and unfinished subdivisions (*Athens Banner-Herald*, 2008). Public opposition to the plan seemed to be the key reason for the change. As reported by journalist Blake Aued (2008b), "removing street lights drew more opposition than any issue since a fight over registering rental tenants five years ago, Commissioner David Lynn said. 'What sets this apart is the broad range of people who called me with concern, with outrage, with outright fear,' he said."

As discussed in chapter 2, there is a long and convoluted history on the use of public street lighting to prevent crime in the United States and Britain. Other countries employ lighting to prevent crime in public places, of course. But to our knowledge, the United States and Britain are the only countries that have evaluated in any rigorous fashion the effectiveness of street lighting in reducing crime. Less rigorous evaluations have been conducted in Australia and the Netherlands (see Challinger, 1992; Vrij and Winkel, 1991).

We base this conclusion on a good number of reviews of the literature (e.g., Cozens et al., 2003; Pease, 1999; Ramsay and Newton, 1991; Tien, O'Donnell, Barnett, and Mirchandani, 1979), as well as our systematic review of the effects of improved street lighting on crime (Farrington and Welsh, 2002a, 2002b, 2006c; Welsh and Farrington, 2004b). Although evaluations may not give the full picture of the extent of the use of street lighting to prevent crime, they (especially the high-quality ones) are the best basis for determinations of effectiveness.

This chapter reviews the scientific evidence on the effectiveness of improved street lighting to prevent crime in public places. It reports on the results of a new update of our systematic review.

Results

Studies were included in the systematic review if they met a number of criteria, including if improved lighting was the main intervention, there was an outcome measure of crime, and the evaluation design was of high methodological quality. (See appendix for full details on the methodology of the systematic review and meta-analysis.) A number of search strategies were employed to locate studies meeting the criteria for inclusion, including searches of electronic bibliographic databases, searches of literature reviews on the effectiveness of improved lighting on crime, and contacts with leading researchers. Thirteen studies met the inclusion criteria, eight from the United States and five from Britain.

American Studies

For the most part, residential neighborhoods were the setting for the intervention. Only four of the eight evaluations specified the degree of improvement in the lighting: by seven times in Milwaukee, four times in Atlanta, three times in Fort Worth, and two times in Portland (see table 6.1). However, the description of the lighting in other cases (e.g., "high-intensity street lighting" in Harrisburg and New Orleans) suggests that there was a marked improvement in the degree of illumination. Only in Indianapolis was the improved street lighting confounded with another concurrent intervention, and it was sometimes possible to disentangle this.

The control area was often adjacent to the experimental area. Hence, similar decreases in crime in experimental and control areas could reflect diffusion of benefits rather than no effect of improved lighting. In most cases, the reports noted that the control area was similar to the experimental area in sociodemographic factors or crime rates. However, none of the evaluations attempted to control for any prior noncomparability of experimental and control areas. Only one evaluation (Portland) included an adjacent area and a comparable nonadjacent control area. (As discussed in chapter 4, this is the best design to assess displacement of crime and diffusion of crime prevention benefits.)

The outcome measure of crime was always based on police records before and after the improved street lighting. The Indianapolis evaluation was based on calls for service to the police, many of which did not clearly involve crimes (e.g., calls for "disturbance"). Only the Atlanta and Milwaukee studies provided total, nighttime, and daytime crimes. The Portland, Kansas City, Harrisburg, and New Orleans studies measured only nighttime crimes, and the Fort Worth and Indianapolis studies reported only total crimes.

As shown in table 6.1, improved street lighting was considered to have a desirable effect on crime in four evaluations: Atlanta, Milwaukee, Fort Worth, and Kansas City. In all four cases, the odds ratio was 1.24 or greater, which corresponds to a 19% decrease in crimes or better.

Table 6.1

American Street Lighting Evaluations

Author, Publication Date, Location	Context of Intervention and Increase in Lighting	Other Interventions	Outcome Measure	Follow-up Period	Results and Diffusion/ Displacement
Atlanta Regional Commission (1974), Atlanta, GA	City center; 4×	None	Crime (robbery, assault, and burglary)	12 months	Desirable effect; no displacement
Department of Intergovernmental Fiscal Liaison(1974), Milwaukee, WI	Residential and commercial area; 7×	None	Crime (property and person categories)	12 months	Desirable effect; some displacement
Inskeep and Goff (1974), Portland, OR	Residential neighborhood (high crime); 2×	None	Crime (robbery, assault, and burglary)	6 or 11 months	Null effect; displacement and diffusion did not occur
Wright et al. (1974), Kansas City, MO	Residential and commercial areas; n.a.	None	Crime (violent and property offenses)	12 months	Desirable effect (for violence); some displacement
Harrisburg Police Department (1976), Harrisburg, PA	Residential neighborhood; n.a.	None	Crime (violent and property offenses)	12 months	Null effect; no displacement
Sternhell (1977), New Orleans, LA	Residential and commercial areas; n.a.	None	Crime (burglary, vehicle theft, and assault)	29 months	Null effect; no displacement
Lewis and Sullivan (1979), Fort Worth, TX	Residential neighborhood; 3×	None	Crime (total)	12 months	Desirable effect; possible displacement
Quinet and Nunn (1998), Indianapolis, IN	Residential neighborhood; n.a.	Police initiatives	Calls for service (violent and property crime)	7–10 months	Null effect; no displacement

Notes: n.a. = not available.

Improved street lighting was most clearly effective in reducing crimes in the Fort Worth evaluation. Crimes decreased by 22% in the experimental area and increased by 9% in the control area (Lewis and Sullivan, 1979). Because crime in the whole city stayed constant (a decrease of 1%), it might be argued that some crime had been displaced from the experimental to the adjacent control area. In the experimental area, property crime decreased, but violent crime did not.

In the other four evaluations, the improved street lighting was considered to have a null effect on crime (evidence of no effect). For example, in Portland, there was little evidence that improved street lighting had led to any reduction in nighttime crime. The analysis of this project was complicated by the fact that one set of experimental, adjacent, and control areas was followed up for 11 months before and after, and another set was followed up for 6 months before and after (Inskeep and Goff, 1974).[1] In general, changes in crime in the experimental areas were similar to and not more desirable than changes in crime in the other areas.

The results of the meta-analysis of all eight U.S. studies yield an odds ratio of 1.08, which was not significant. Overall, crime decreased by 7% in experimental areas compared with control areas.

The key dimension on which the eight effect sizes differed seemed to be whether they were based on data for both night and day (Atlanta, Milwaukee, Fort Worth, and Indianapolis) or for night only (the other four studies). For the four night/day studies, the average effect size was a significant odds ratio of 1.28, meaning that crime decreased by 22% in experimental areas compared with control areas. For the night-only studies, the odds ratio was 1.01, indicating no effect on crime. Therefore, the eight U.S. studies could be divided into two blocks of four, one block showing that crime reduced after improved street lighting and the other block showing that it did not. Surprisingly, evidence of a reduction in crime was only obtained when both daytime and nighttime crimes were measured, although this feature may be a proxy for some other aspect of the different evaluation studies.

Unfortunately, all the U.S. evaluations (except the Indianapolis one) are now rather dated, because they were all carried out in the 1970s. More recent evaluations of the effect of improved street lighting need to be conducted. We now turn to the British evaluations, which were all published in the 1990s.

British Studies

The five British street lighting studies were carried out in a variety of settings, including a parking garage and a market, as well as residential neighborhoods (see table 6.2). Three of the evaluations specified the degree of improvement in lighting: by five times in Stoke-on-Trent and by two times in Bristol (approximately) and Dudley. Control areas were usually located close to experimental areas. The outcome measure of crime was based on police records for three studies and on victim surveys in the other two cases (in Dudley and Stoke-on-Trent). Uniquely, the Dudley project also evaluated the impact of improved street lighting using self-reported delinquency surveys of young people. This project also included self-reports of victimization of young people and measures of fear of crime (Painter and Farrington, 2001a).

As shown in table 6.2, improved street lighting was considered to be effective in reducing crime in four studies (Bristol, Birmingham, Dudley, and Stoke-on-Trent). In the fifth study (Dover), the improved lighting was confounded with other improvements, including fencing to restrict access to the parking garage and the construction of an office near the main entrance. The officials considered the crime prevention measures successful because the reduced costs of damage and graffiti paid for the improvements within one year. On the basis of police records, Barry Poyner (1991) concluded that the intervention had reduced thefts *of* vehicles but not thefts *from* vehicles.

In the Birmingham study of city center markets, two six-month periods before the improved lighting were compared with two six-month periods after. There were interventions in one of the control markets that could have led to reductions in crime. Nevertheless, the reduction in thefts from the person in the experimental market after the improved lighting was far greater than in the control markets. The experimental market was large and covered, and its lighting was markedly improved. Barry Poyner and Barry Webb (1997, p. 89) concluded that, "increased levels of illumination appear to have deterred would-be thieves."

In the Dudley study, crime was measured using before-and-after victim surveys in experimental and control areas. Large samples were interviewed: 431 in the experimental area and 448 in the control area. The response rate was 77% in both areas before and 84% after (of those interviewed before). Substantial crime reduction benefits were achieved after

Table 6.2
British Street Lighting Evaluations

Author, Publication Date, Location	Context of Intervention and Increase in Lighting	Other Interventions	Outcome Measure	Follow-up Period	Results and Diffusion/ Displacement
Poyner (1991), Dover	Parking garage (in town center); n.a.	Fencing, office constructed	Crime (total and theft of and from vehicles)	24 months	Desirable effect (for theft of vehicles); no displacement
Shaftoe (1994), Bristol	Residential neighborhood; 2×	None	Crime (total)	12 months	Desirable effect; not measured
Poyner and Webb (1997), Birmingham	City center market; n.a.	None	Thefts	12 months (6 months in each of 2 years)	Desirable effect; no displacement and some diffusion
Painter and Farrington (1997), Dudley	Local authority housing estate; 2×	None	Crime (total and types of offenses)	12 months	Desirable effect; no displacement
Painter and Farrington (1999), Stoke-on-Trent	Local authority housing estate; 5×	None	Crime (total and types of offenses)	12 months	Desirable effect; diffusion, no displacement

Note: n.a. = not available.

one year of the improved street lighting scheme. In the experimental area, the prevalence of all crime decreased by one-quarter (24%), whereas only a marginal decrease (3%) in the prevalence of all crime occurred in the control area. Also, the incidence (average number of victimizations per 100 households) of all crime decreased in both the experimental and control areas: 41% and 15%, respectively. The decrease in the experimental area was found to be significantly greater than the decrease in the control area (Painter and Farrington, 1997).

The Dudley study also evaluated the impact of improved street lighting using a self-reported delinquency survey completed by young people living on the experimental and control estates. Altogether, 307 young people were interviewed in the before survey and 334 in the after survey (Painter and Farrington, 2001a). The self-reported delinquency results were surprisingly similar to the victim survey results. Crime decreased in the experimental area by 35% and in the control area by 14% according to self-reports.[2] No evidence was found that displacement had occurred.

The Stoke study included both adjacent and nonadjacent control areas. This allows for the most accurate measurement of any displacement or diffusion effects. Again, victim surveys were used, with an 84% response rate before and an 89% response rate after (of those interviewed before). The incidence of crime decreased by 43% in the experimental area, 45% in the adjacent area, and only 2% in the control area (Painter and Farrington, 1999). When differences in the pretest victimization rates (prevalence and incidence) in all three areas were controlled for, it was found that the changes in experimental and adjacent areas were significantly greater than in the control area. Police records also showed a decrease in crime of only 2% in the larger police area containing all the project areas. It was concluded that improved street lighting had caused a decrease in crime in the experimental area and that there had been a diffusion of benefits to the adjacent area, which was not clearly delimited from it.

Results of the meta-analysis of the five British studies confirm these conclusions. Total crimes reduced significantly after improved lighting in Bristol, Birmingham, Dudley, and Stoke-on-Trent. When the odds ratios from the five studies were combined, crimes decreased by 38% in experimental areas compared with control areas (odds ratio = 1.62).

In conclusion, these more recent British studies agree in showing that improved lighting reduces crime. They did not find that nighttime crimes decreased more than daytime crimes, suggesting that a "community pride" theory may be more applicable than a "deterrence/surveillance" theory.

Crime Type

We were also able to investigate the effects of improved street lighting on different types of crime. Violent crimes were measured in 9 evaluations, and property crimes were measured in 11 evaluations. Lighting improvements were followed by a significant reduction in property crimes, for a mean odds ratio of 1.20. This corresponds to a 17% decrease in property crimes in experimental areas compared to control areas. In contrast, lighting improvements lead to a small and nonsignificant reduction in violent crimes, with an odds ratio of 1.10 or a 9% decrease.

Pooled Effects

From the 13 evaluations, it was concluded that improved street lighting had a significant desirable effect on crime, with a weighted mean odds ratio of 1.27. This means that crimes decreased by 21% in experimental areas compared with control areas.[3] Interestingly, both nighttime and daytime crimes were measured in all five British studies and four of the eight U.S. studies. The nine night/day studies also showed a significant desirable effect of improved lighting on crime (odds ratio = 1.43), an almost one-third (30%) decrease in crimes in experimental areas compared with control areas. However, the studies that only measured nighttime crime showed no effect (odds ratio = 1.01).

Figure 6.1 summarizes the results of all 13 studies in a forest graph. It shows the odds ratio for total crime measured in each study plus its 95% confidence interval. The studies are ordered according to their magnitudes of their odds ratios. It can be seen that only three studies (Portland, New Orleans, and Indianapolis) had odds ratios less than 1, meaning that improved street lighting was followed by an increase in crime, and in no case was this increase significant. The other 10 studies had odds ratios greater than 1, meaning that improved street lighting was followed by a decrease in crime, and in 6 cases this decrease was significant (or nearly so, in the case of Atlanta). Therefore, the hypothesis that more lighting causes more crime can be firmly rejected.

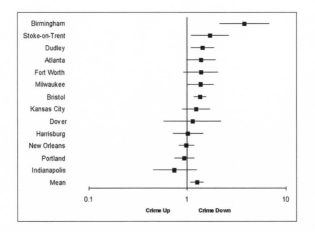

Figure 6.1 Meta-Analysis Results of Improved Street Lighting Evaluations
Note: Odds ratios on logarithmic scale.

Discussion and Conclusions

Results were mixed for the eight U.S. evaluation studies. Four found that improved street lighting was effective in reducing crime, whereas the other four found that it was not effective. Why the studies produced different results was not obvious, although there was a tendency for effective studies to measure both daytime and nighttime crimes and for ineffective studies to measure only nighttime crimes. However, all except one (Indianapolis) of these American evaluations date from the 1970s.

Five more recent British evaluation studies showed that lighting improvements led to decreases in crime. Furthermore, in two studies (Dudley and Stoke-on-Trent), cost-benefit analyses showed that the financial savings from reduced crimes greatly exceeded the financial costs of the improved street lighting (Painter and Farrington, 2001b). In the case of Dudley, total monetary benefits were 6.2 times as great as the total costs of the project, including the full capital expenditure. In other words, for every £1 that was spent on the improved lighting scheme, £6.19 was saved by the local council and victims of crime in one year. In the same one-year timeframe, the Stoke lighting scheme produced a slightly lower return on investment: for each £1, £5.43 was saved by the local council and crime victims. These returns on investment are even more impressive because in each case the capital costs of installing the lighting improvements were taken into account in full, instead of the standard practice of including only the annual debt payment on the capital expenditure calculated over a reasonable life expectancy of the program.

Because the British studies also did not find that nighttime crimes decreased more than daytime crimes, a theory of street lighting focusing on its role in increasing community pride and informal social control may be more plausible than a theory focusing on increased surveillance and deterrence. The results were also consistent with the hypothesis that improved street lighting was most effective in reducing crime in stable, homogeneous communities.

It was speculated that improved lighting may improve community pride only in relatively stable homogeneous communities (probably because of cohesiveness), not in areas with a heterogeneous population mix and high residential mobility. The lack of systematic information on residential mobility makes it difficult to draw clear conclusions about whether improved street lighting was more effective in reducing crime in stable, homogeneous communities than in unstable, heterogeneous communities. Nevertheless, none of the 10 studies that could be included in this analysis clearly contradicted this hypothesis, and 4 (Dudley, Stoke-on-Trent, Harrisburg, and Fort Worth) were clearly concordant with it.[4] This finding is again in agreement with the hypothesis that increased community pride causes decreased crime. It also suggests that social disorganization theory (see chapter 3) might be useful in designing situational crime prevention schemes.

An alternative hypothesis is that increased community pride comes first, causing improved street lighting on one hand and reduced crime on the other, with no causal effect of improved lighting on crime. It is difficult to exclude this hypothesis on the basis of most published evaluation reports. However, it can be excluded in the two evaluations (Dudley and Stoke-on-Trent) in which one of us (Farrington) was involved.

In Dudley, there had been no marked changes on the experimental estate for many years. The tenants on this and other local authority housing estates had complained about the poor lighting for some time, and this was the reason the local authority decided to improve the lighting on the experimental estate. The improvement was very obvious, and tenants thought that their quality of life had been improved (Painter and Farrington, 1997). This stimulated the tenants' association on the experimental estate to obtain £10 million (approximately US$15 million) from the Department of the Environment for a program of neighborhood improvements over the next few years. The improvement in lighting on the experimental estate also stimulated the tenants' association on the control estate to petition the local authority to improve their lighting.

In Dudley, it was clear that the improved lighting occurred first, led to increased community pride, and acted as a catalyst for further environmental improvements. A similar chain of events happened in Stoke-on-Trent. Although we cannot be sure that the same causal ordering occurred in all other street lighting evaluations, it might be concluded that in at least some studies, improved lighting caused increased community pride and decreased crime.

On the whole, convincing results were found on the important issue of displacement and diffusion. Only 3 of the 13 studies reported some or possible evidence that lighting improvements caused crimes to be displaced to the surrounding areas. The other nine studies reported no evidence of territorial or geographical displacement, with two of these (Birmingham and Stoke) also reporting at least some evidence of diffusion of crime prevention benefits to nearby areas that did not receive the intervention.

The policy implications of research on improved street lighting have been well articulated by British criminologist Ken Pease (1999). He pointed out that situational crime prevention involved the modification of environments so that crime needed more effort, required more risk, and offered lower rewards. The first step in any crime reduction program required a careful analysis of situations and how they affected potential offenders and potential victims. The second step involved implementing crime reduction interventions. Whether improved street lighting was likely to be effective in reducing crime would depend on characteristics of situations and other concurrent situational interventions. Efforts to reduce crime should take account of the fact that crime tends to be concentrated among certain people and in certain locations, rather than being evenly distributed throughout a community.

The British studies show that improved lighting can be effective in reducing crime in some circumstances. Exactly what are the optimal circumstances is not clear at present, and this needs to be established by future evaluation research. However, improved street lighting should be considered as a potential strategy in any crime reduction program in coordination with other intervention strategies. Depending on the analysis of the crime problem, improved street lighting could often be implemented as a feasible, inexpensive, and effective method of reducing crime.

In the next chapter, we review and assess the effectiveness of other forms of surveillance to prevent crime in public places.

Security Guards, Place Managers, and Defensible Space

7

One of the main goals of this book is to assess the effectiveness of the full range of surveillance measures that are used to prevent crime in public places. Closed-circuit television (CCTV) and improved street lighting are the most well-developed surveillance measures currently in use. This is true at least in terms of the body of work that has been carried out over the years to evaluate these measures.

Other widely used surveillance measures that perform a crime prevention function in public places include security guards, place managers, and defensible space. Security guards in particular represent a growth industry. In the United States, the most recent estimates suggest that there are more than one million security guards, or about three for every two sworn police officers (Cunningham, Strauchs, and Van Meter, 1990). A substantial and growing number of these security guards work in public settings (Sklansky, 2006).

In Boston, for example, a number of private security firms are contracted by the city to patrol public places. One of these companies is Naratoone, which is responsible for the security of more than 100 public housing communities and low-income apartment buildings around the city. In a few short years, the company tripled its security force to more than 150. What makes this company different from other private firms working in public places in the city is that in addition to traditional security officers, it employs "special" police officers, who are "armed and licensed by the Boston Police Department and who have limited arrest powers" (Swidey, 2006). There are now more than 200 of these special police officers working throughout the city (Cramer, 2008). The measure was taken as part of an effort to bolster a recent decline—almost 10% between 2001 and 2006—in the numbers of Boston police officers. Despite generally positive reviews, some concerns have been raised about these special officers exceeding their powers (Cramer, 2008; Swidey, 2006). This comes in addition to the long-standing concern that "private police" operate with far less oversight than public police (Manning, 1999).

Some Boston companies, like GTI Properties, have expanded their security details to include public places that border their private premises, including streets, street corners, and parks. This, too, is part of an effort to shore up the reduced numbers of police officers in the city. Unlike the special police officers, these security officers are unarmed, do not have arrest powers, and are "careful not to take on [police] officers' responsibilities" (Smalley, 2006). Instead, they resort to warning people about loitering outside their buildings, sometimes with the threat of calling the police, using spotlights to reveal untoward activities taking place in dark alleyways, and using video surveillance cameras to capture criminal activities in progress that can then be shared with the police.

Little is known, however—and certainly much less than CCTV and improved street lighting (see chapters 5 and 6, respectively)—about the effectiveness of security guards, place managers, and defensible space in preventing crime in public places. For this reason, these forms of public area surveillance are grouped together in this chapter.

To return to Derek Cornish and Ronald Clarke's (2003) classification of situational crime prevention, each of these measures falls under one of the three types of surveillance they outlined: formal surveillance, place managers (or surveillance by employees), and natural surveillance. These types are designed to increase offenders' risks associated with committing a crime. Security guards, like CCTV, are a technique of formal surveillance. Here, the aim is to produce a "deterrent threat to potential offenders." *Place managers* refers to persons such as bus drivers, parking lot attendants, train conductors, and others who perform a surveillance function by virtue of their position of employment. Unlike security personnel, however, the task of surveillance for these employees is secondary to their other job duties. Defensible space involves changes to the built environment. Like improved street lighting, it is a technique of natural surveillance. This type of surveillance involves efforts to "capitalize upon the 'natural' surveillance provided by people going about their everyday business" (Clarke, 1997, pp. 20–21).

This chapter reviews the scientific evidence on the crime prevention effectiveness of these three other major forms of public area surveillance. It reports on the results of systematic reviews that we conducted. Studies were included in the three systematic reviews if they met a number of criteria, including if the surveillance measure in question was the main intervention, there was an outcome measure of crime, and the evaluation design was of high methodological quality. A number of search strategies were employed to locate studies meeting the criteria for inclusion, including searches of electronic bibliographic databases, searches of literature reviews on the effectiveness of the surveillance measures, and contacts with leading researchers. (The appendix provides full details on the methodology of the reviews.) Across the three systematic reviews, only 12 evaluation studies met the criteria for inclusion: 5 for security guards, 2 for place managers, and 5 for defensible space. These small number of studies, along with a few other issues we discuss, made the use of meta-analytic techniques to analyze results undesirable. However, this does not hamper our ability to draw conclusions about the effectiveness of these forms of public area surveillance. Importantly, our conclusions here, as in other chapters, are based on the best available scientific evidence.

Security Guards

The five evaluations of security guards were carried out in four different countries: two in the United States and one each in Canada, the Netherlands, and the United Kingdom (see table 7.1). Two (Kenney, 1986; Pennell, Curtis, Henderson, and Tayman, 1989) are more correctly referred to as urban citizen patrols. Each of these involved the group known as the Guardian Angels. Although both security guards and citizen patrols perform a formal surveillance function, this is where their similarities end. For this reason, we discuss them separately. We begin with the results of our review of the three evaluations of security guards.

Table 7.1
Evaluations of Security Guards

Author, Publication Date, Location	Type of Intervention and Context	Other Interventions	Outcome Measure	Follow-up Period	Results and Diffusion/ Displacement
Kenney (1986), New York, NY	Urban citizen patrols (Guardian Angels); subway stations	None	Crime (total and multiple offenses)	n.a.	Null effect; not measured
Pennell et al. (1986, 1989), San Diego, CA	Urban citizen patrols (Guardian Angels); city redevelopment area	Police foot patrol	Violent and property crimes	30 months	Desirable effect (for property crimes); not measured
Laycock and Austin (1992), Basingstoke, U.K.	Security guards; car parks	Fencing, defensible space	Theft of vehicles	1 year	Desirable effect; no displacement
Hesseling (1995), Rotterdam, Netherlands	Security guards; car parks	None	Theft from vehicles	2 years	Null effect; displacement occurred (in 4 of 5 control areas)
Barclay et al. (1996), Vancouver, Canada	Security guards; commuter car park	Media campaign	Theft of vehicles	4 months	Desirable effect; little or no displacement

Note: n.a. = not available.

Each of the security guard studies were carried out in car parks that were experiencing high rates of vehicle crimes. In two cases, security guards were supplemented with other (secondary) interventions. In the Basingstoke study, conducted by U.K. Home Office researchers Gloria Laycock and Claire Austin (1992), fencing was installed around a good portion of the car park, and a number of defensible space practices were implemented, including pruning the trees in front of some houses that bordered the car park and building a public footpath alongside it. In the Vancouver study, conducted by Canadian criminologists Paul Barclay, Jennifer Buckley, Paul and Patricia Brantingham, and Terry Whinn-Yates (1996), a media campaign preceded the implementation of the security patrols. All three of the evaluations measured vehicle crimes, and the length of follow-up ranged from a low of 4 months to a high of 2 years.

The Basingstoke and Vancouver schemes were highly effective in reducing vehicle thefts, and in both programs the researchers recorded little or no displacement of vehicle thefts into surrounding areas. However, the implementation of security guards in a number of car parks in the inner city of Rotterdam produced no measurable change in thefts from vehicles over a two-year period. Evidence of spatial displacement was recorded in four of the five control areas. From interviews with offenders and an analysis of the deployment of the security guards, Dutch criminologist René Hesseling (1995) concluded that the Rotterdam scheme was not intense enough to deal with the volume of motivated offenders.

The program evaluated by Barclay and colleagues (1996) is particularly noteworthy. Bicycle-mounted security guard patrols were introduced in Vancouver's largest park-and-ride commuter car park to deal with increased rates of vehicle thefts. An analysis of the layout of the parking lot and surrounding area revealed that formal surveillance was the most viable option. Poor visibility into the car park and no nearby shops or other establishments with a regular flow of pedestrians limited the use of natural surveillance measures. The security patrols operated for one month and, as noted, were preceded by a media campaign to inform the public about the program. Three months after the program ended, there was an average of 14 fewer vehicle thefts per month in the experimental area compared to an average of 4.5 more vehicle thefts per month in the surrounding area, which served as the control. An analysis of displacement showed that little if any of this increase in vehicle thefts in the control area was a result of them being displaced from the experimental area.

Urban Citizen Patrols

Like their security guard counterparts, urban citizen patrols seek to furnish a deterrent threat to potential offenders and can be classified as a technique of formal surveillance. Citizen dissatisfaction with the police response to escalating crime problems in their immediate neighborhood, wider community, or city is often the main reason for the development of these groups. The best known group is the Guardian Angels. It is also the only known urban citizen patrol group that has been rigorously evaluated to assess its impact on crime.

The Guardian Angels organization began operations in 1979 as a small group of citizen volunteers riding the New York City subway system with the intention of "deterring crimes by their presence and making citizen arrests when serious crimes were observed" (Kenney, 1986, p. 482). During the 1980s, the Guardian Angels grew to include thousands of members across the country. Currently, the Guardian Angels have more than 90 chapters in operation around the world. Their volunteer, unarmed citizen patrols are now complemented by community education seminars on violence prevention as well as an Internet safety program called Cyber Angels, which is meant as a response to citizen calls for protection from online threats (Guardian Angels, 2007).

The two evaluations of the Guardian Angels took place in New York City and San Diego in the mid-1980s (see table 7.1). Kenney (1986) found that they had no appreciable effect on crime in New York City's subway system over an unspecified follow-up period. He noted that the evaluation was severely hampered by the overall small number of criminal incidents that occurred on the subway.[1] Displacement was not measured.

In San Diego, Pennell and colleagues (1989) found that the introduction of patrols by the Guardian Angels in a downtown redevelopment area was effective in reducing property crime but had no effect on violent crime over a 30-month follow-up period. Property crime went down 25% in the experimental area, compared to a 15% reduction in the control area. Violent crime also went down in both areas, but the control area experienced a much larger reduction than the experimental area (42% versus 22%). The authors speculated that factors other than the patrols might explain the reduction in violent crime in the experimental area. This view was borne out by the results of further analyses showing that there was no significant association between the number of patrols and police-reported violent crime. Complicating matters further (for both property and violent crime reductions in the experimental area), police foot patrols were initiated in the redevelopment area at the same time as the Guardian Angels patrols. The authors did not measure displacement or diffusion.

Place Managers

As already noted, place managers differ from security guards (as well as citizen patrols) in that surveillance is not the primary duty of their employment. In the case of parking lot attendants, for example, they are first and foremost responsible for parking and retrieving vehicles for customers and collecting money for this service. The secondary surveillance function they perform comes about from their presence and ability to intervene, thus presenting a deterrent threat to potential offenders. Bus drivers, train conductors, and concierges (or doormen) are examples of other place managers who work in public settings.

Disappointingly, only two evaluations of the effects of place managers on crime in public places could be included in our systematic review. Both of these were carried out in the United Kingdom some years ago (see table 7.2). We found a number of other evaluations of place managers in our search for studies, but they were all excluded because they did not meet the criteria for inclusion. By and large, this was because they used weak evaluation designs, often a simple before-and-after, no-control condition design.[2] We now turn to a description of the two place manager studies.

High crime levels and generally poor security in the London borough of Brent's South Kilburn public housing estate led to the introduction in 1984 of a concierge system in one of its high-rise residential towers (Gloucester House). The concierge scheme, which operated from 8 A.M. to 11 P.M., performed three main functions: receptionist services (e.g., answering calls), general assistance to residents, and maintenance of block security by controlling access through the main entrance (Skilton, 1988, p. 14).

Compared to a matched neighboring residential high-rise housing block on the estate (Hereford House),[3] the experimental site showed a number of benefits over a one-year follow-up period, including fewer repairs to communal areas (5 versus 131) and elevators (28 versus 75) (from a reduction in vandalism) and less revenue lost due to vacant flats. Neither

Table 7.2

Evaluations of Place Managers

Author, Publication Date, Location	Type of Intervention and Context	Other Interventions	Outcome Measure	Follow-up Period	Results and Diffusion/ Displacement
Skilton (1988), London borough of Brent, U.K.	Concierge system; public housing estate (South Kilburn)	None	Vandalism	1 year	Desirable effect; not measured
Poyner (1991), Dover, U.K.	Taxi business; parking garage	Lighting, fencing, access control	Vehicle crimes	2 years	Uncertain effect; no displacement

displacement nor diffusion of benefits was measured. A cost-benefit analysis showed that the financial savings from a reduction in vandalism and associated improvements exceeded the financial costs of the concierge program; that is, for £1 that was spent on the scheme, £1.44 was saved to the borough of Brent in one year.[4]

In the other study, carried out by Barry Poyner (1991), place managers took the form of a taxi company operating out of a multilevel parking garage in the southeastern British city of Dover. The parking garage was experiencing a range of crime problems, most notably thefts of and from vehicles. City officials, in consultation with a crime prevention police officer, implemented a package of situational crime prevention measures. The major intervention involved constructing an office at the main entrance of the parking garage and leasing it to a taxi company that operated from the site. The taxi business was open most hours on the weekend and from 8 A.M. to midnight on the other days. Other measures included lighting improvements at the main entrance, installation of fencing at the ground level, and an exit-only door to restrict access to customers of the parking garage.

To evaluate the effectiveness of this initiative, the author used as control areas two nearby open parking lots that had a similar number of parking spaces and used the same payment system as the garage. The open lots had about half the number of vehicle crimes as the parking garage in the two years prior to the start of the program. Two years after the program began, police-reported vehicle crimes were down by half in both the experimental area (50%) and the control area (49%). Because the author did not investigate whether the control area's reduction in vehicle crime resulted from a diffusion of benefits from the targeted site, it is difficult to say whether this scheme was indeed effective. Poyner found no evidence that vehicle crimes were displaced to the control parking lots.

Defensible Space

Defensible space involves design changes to the built environment to maximize the natural surveillance of open spaces (e.g., streets, parks, parking lots) afforded by people going about their day-to-day activities. Some of these design changes include the construction of street barricades, the redesign of walkways, and the installation of windows. Defensible space can also involve more mundane techniques, such as removing objects that obscure lines of sight from shelves or windows of convenience stores and removing or pruning bushes in front of homes so that residents may have a clear view of the outside.

In the context of public settings, we found five evaluations of defensible space that met the criteria for inclusion in our review. Four of these evaluations were carried out in the United States and the other one in the United Kingdom (see table 7.3). Each of the U.S. studies involved street closures or other traffic modifications in mostly inner-city neighborhoods. The U.K. study involved building design changes on public housing estates. Two of the studies (Armitage, 2000; Donnelly and Kimble, 1997) used other interventions. For most of the studies, effectiveness was measured with a range of violent and property crimes, and follow-up periods lasted between one and three years.

All of the evaluations reported a desirable effect on at least some of the crimes that were measured; none found that crime increased in the experimental area (compared to the control area). In the Miami Shores study, conducted by Randall Atlas and William LeBlanc (1994), 67 street closures and barricades were constructed across the city in an effort to curb crime and traffic problems. Two adjacent municipalities were selected

Table 7.3
Evaluations of Defensible Space

Author, Publication Date, Location	Type of Intervention and Context	Other Interventions	Outcome Measure	Follow-up Period	Results and Diffusion/ Displacement
Atlas and LeBlanc (1994), Miami Shores, FL	Street closures and barricades; citywide	None	Violent and property crimes	2 years	Desirable effect (for burglary, larceny, theft of vehicles); not measured
Donnelly and Kimble (1997), Dayton, OH	Street closures; inner-city neighborhoods	Media campaign	Crime (total and multiple offenses)	2 years	Desirable effect; some evidence of displacement and diffusion
Wagner (1997), St. Louis, MO	Traffic modification; inner-city neighborhood	None	Violent and property crimes (part I)	1 year	Desirable effect; not measured
Lasley (1998), Los Angeles, CA	Street barricades; inner-city neighborhoods	None	Violent and property crimes (part I)	3 years	Desirable effect (for homicides and assaults); no displacement
Armitage (2000), West Yorkshire, U.K.	Secured by design; public housing estates	Physical security, access control	Crime (total and multiple offenses)	n.a.	Desirable effect; not measured

Note: n.a. = not available.

as control areas: Miami-Dade County and the city of Miami. Compared to the control areas, Miami Shores experienced a significant decrease in burglary, larceny, and theft of vehicles two years after the program was implemented, but no change was observed in robberies and aggravated assaults over the same time frame. Displacement was not measured. The authors offer the following view on how the barricades and street closures might have produced the observed crime reductions:

> The reduction in crime may not have been a direct result
> of the fact that barricades reduced traffic and discouraged
> nonresidents from cruising Miami Shores' neighborhoods.
> Rather, the barricades may have made residents feel safer and
> more comfortable walking around their neighborhoods, thereby
> increasing natural surveillance. This natural surveillance may
> have, in turn, deterred would-be criminals from victimizing
> residents. (Atlas and LeBlanc, 1994, p. 144)

In an evaluation of a traffic barrier scheme in Los Angeles, criminologist James Lasley (1998) found that violent crimes went down, but there was no change in property crimes. Known as Operation Cul de Sac (because the barriers changed through roads into cul-de-sacs), the Los Angeles Police Department installed traffic barriers in a 10-block area of inner-city neighborhoods that were experiencing heightened levels of gang-perpetrated violence, including drive-by shootings, homicides, and assaults. The remaining patrol division areas that surrounded the targeted site served as the controls. In the two years that the traffic barriers were in place, the experimental area, compared to the control areas, experienced significant reductions in homicide and assault, but no changes were observed in property crimes (i.e., burglary, vehicles crimes, larceny, and bicycle theft). During this period of time, the author found no evidence of displacement of crimes to surrounding neighborhoods. The situation changed once the traffic barriers were removed. In the following year, homicides and assaults increased in the experimental area, and in the control areas homicides increased and assaults remained constant. At least for homicides, this provided further support that the program had a desirable effect (Lasley, 1998, p. 3).

Similar efforts to close streets and modify traffic were also judged to be effective in high-crime neighborhoods in St. Louis, Missouri, and Dayton, Ohio. Allen Wagner (1997) found that the St. Louis neighborhood that implemented traffic modifications had a lower rate of increase in the overall crime rate than the adjacent (control) neighborhood. Patrick Donnelly and Charles Kimble (1997) found that a Dayton neighborhood that implemented street closures produced substantial reductions in both property and violent crimes compared to the control areas. Displacement was not measured in the St. Louis study. In the Dayton study, the authors found some evidence that crimes were displaced to five of the eight control areas, along with some evidence of a diffusion of crime prevention benefits in the other three control areas.

The most recent defensible space evaluation, conducted by British criminologist Rachel Armitage (2000), took a different approach from the others. Here, defensible space principles, along with other situational crime prevention techniques (e.g., physical security, access control), were integrated in the building of public and other housing. The program is known as Secured by Design (SBD), a national award program run by the Association of Chief Police Officers in the United Kingdom, which aims to "encourage housing developers to design out crime, with a particular emphasis on domestic burglary, at the planning stage" (Armitage, 2000, p. 1).

The evaluation design involved 50 matched public housing estates in West Yorkshire, 25 with the SBD program and 25 without it. Over an unspecified follow-up period, the prevalence of total crime (the proportion of homes that were victimized at least once) was almost statistically significantly lower on the experimental estates compared to the controls (37% versus 44%). Displacement was not measured. Importantly, because the SBD program incorporated multiple measures and no single measure seemed to be more important than the other, it is difficult to isolate the effects of defensible space on crime. Subsequent research by the author (Armitage, 2006, 2007) investigated this issue and found that controlling access routes to the housing estates (e.g., footpaths) and reducing the level of pedestrian and vehicular traffic through and around the estate, thereby reducing its "permeability," was associated with a decreased risk of crime.

Discussion and Conclusions

The reviews revealed generally favorable results across the three different types of public area surveillance. There is fairly strong and consistent evidence that the defensible space technique of street closures or barricades is effective in preventing crime in inner-city neighborhoods. Less conclusive statements can be made about the efficacy of security guards and place managers. This has everything to do with the small number of high-quality evaluations that have been carried out on these measures. In the case of security guards, the weight of the evidence suggests that it is a promising technique of formal surveillance when implemented in car parks and targeted at vehicle crimes. The surveillance technique of place managers appears to be of unknown effectiveness in preventing crime in public places.

As with CCTV and improved street lighting, the setting in which the intervention took place, the crime type targeted, and the nature or characteristics of the intervention are important to our conclusions here about the state of what works for these other major forms of public area surveillance. This was particularly important for defensible space. A blanket statement that "it works" is not justified. With only one known high-quality evaluation of SBD (Armitage, 2000), it is not possible at this time to make an assessment of its effectiveness. However, the other four evaluations of defensible space represent a largely uniform subset of this surveillance measure. Each implemented street closures or barricades, three of the four were carried out in high-crime inner-city neighborhoods (the other was implemented across the city), and each produced desirable effects on overall crime or a specific crime type (violence in one case and property in the other).

One of the interesting points emerging from the evaluations of street closures or barricades concerns an understanding of the mechanism that explains why this intervention has the effect it does. For some, the effectiveness of street closures or barricades to reduce crime depends on its physical presence. Derek Cornish and Ronald Clarke (2003) refer to this as deflecting offenders away from crime targets. For others, the effect on crime is seen as a product of increased natural surveillance on the part of residents, who now feel safer being outside. In all of the evaluations, the authors argued that natural surveillance caused the reduction in crime. Support for this position came from improvements in residents' perceptions of crime.

Our conclusion that security guards represent a promising technique of formal surveillance when implemented in car parks and targeted at vehicle crimes is based on two evaluations, both of which produced sizable reductions in vehicle crimes in this public setting, as well as the larger body of research on this topic. Promising programs are those in which the level of certainty from the available scientific evidence is too low to support generalizable conclusions, but there is some empirical basis for predicting that further research could support such conclusions (Farrington, Gottfredson, Sherman, and Welsh, 2006, p. 18).

One potential drawback to this promising designation is that both of the effective programs used other (secondary) interventions: a media campaign in the study by Barclay and colleagues (1996) and fencing and defensible space measures in the study by Laycock and Austin (1992). Another potential drawback is that the other security guard study included in our review (Hesseling, 1995) did not produce a desirable effect on vehicle crimes in car parks. Nevertheless, the promising nature of security guards still seems valid, if only because we are not recommending wider use but instead calling for further experimentation. Unfortunately, the two urban citizen patrol studies do not add much to our knowledge base on the effectiveness of formal surveillance.

More straightforward is our conclusion that the surveillance technique of place managers appears to be of unknown effectiveness in preventing crime in public places. Only two evaluations met the criteria for inclusion in the systematic review, and they were carried out in different public settings (public housing estate or parking garage) and targeted at different crimes (vandalism or vehicle crimes). Furthermore, the study by Poyner (1991) in a parking garage produced an uncertain effect on crime. This form of surveillance could also benefit from further experimentation. Given the state of the scientific evidence at this point in time, it may be more fruitful to give precedence to other surveillance measures, such as security guards.

Unfortunately, little can be said about the economic efficiency of any one of these three major forms of public area surveillance. Skilton (1988) carried out the only cost-benefit analysis. He found that a place manager scheme—in the form of a concierge system in a public housing estate—produced monetary benefits that exceeded program costs by a ratio of almost 1.5 to 1. Additionally, little can be said about the displacement of crime or diffusion of crime prevention benefits associated with these forms of surveillance. These are important issues that need to be investigated as part of future evaluations.

It bears repeating that grouping these other forms of public area surveillance in this chapter is not meant to suggest that they are any less important than CCTV or street lighting. Rather, to return to the point in this chapter's introduction, this was done because much less is known about the state of evaluation research on these measures.

In the next chapter, we explore key policy choices and challenges that face U.S. cities in the use of these and the other major forms of surveillance to prevent crime in public places.

Part III

Policy Choices and Challenges

Safer Streets, Safer Cities: Policy Choices for America

8

On the basis of the highest quality research evidence available of the effects on crime of the five major forms of public area surveillance, a few general conclusions can be drawn. First, closed-circuit television (CCTV), improved street lighting, and the defensible space practice of street closures or barricades seem to be effective in preventing crime. Second, security guards are promising in preventing crime. Third, place managers appear to be of unknown effectiveness. For city managers, police chiefs, urban planners, business owners, or others, this may be useful information if a decision needs to be made about implementing one or the other measure. (Hopefully, as Mark Moore [2002] argued in another context, a cost-effectiveness analysis or comparative cost-benefit analysis would also be carried out to inform this decision.[1]) For some, this information may be far too limited.

What may prove more helpful to policy makers and practitioners is information about the specific conditions under which these surveillance measures are most effective in preventing crime. The present research shows that CCTV is effective in preventing crime in car parks; improved street lighting is effective in city and town centers and residential/public housing communities; and the defensible space practice of street closures or barricades is effective in inner-city neighborhoods. (Just as important are those conditions under which surveillance measures are not effective. We discuss this shortly.)

Also of importance is evidence that shows that CCTV and improved street lighting are more effective in reducing property (especially vehicle) crimes than in reducing violent crimes. Street closure or barricade schemes are effective in reducing both property and violent crimes. The weight of the evidence suggests that security guards are promising when implemented in car parks and targeted at vehicle crimes.

Striking a Balance between Crime Reduction and Social Costs

Andrew von Hirsch (2000) argues that two major issues confront the "proper uses and limits" of surveillance for crime prevention in public places. His discussion takes place in the context of CCTV, but it is relevant to the other forms of public area surveillance that we cover in this book. The first issue pertains to privacy concerns. In chapter 2, we expanded on privacy concerns to include other social costs that may infringe on public interests or violate legal or constitutional protections; we return to these points here. The second issue concerns the matter of the "legitimising role of crime prevention," or as von Hirsch (2000, p. 61) posits, "To what extent does crime prevention legitimise impinging on any interests of privacy or anonymity in public space?" We investigate this matter here.

Our analysis begins with CCTV. In car parks, the one setting in which CCTV is effective in preventing crime (specifically vehicle crime), there may be little resistance to the installation of CCTV cameras. In part, this is because this public space is used for one rather inconsequential purpose—parking vehicles. It is also the case that a car park is a well-defined and clearly marked physical space, meaning that individuals know that it is a car park and can choose whether to park their vehicle there (providing there are other alternatives). These points stand in sharp contrast with how individuals come into contact with CCTV in other public settings (see following discussion).

One could take issue with CCTV cameras in public car parks. For the period of time that the vehicle is parked, including leaving and returning to the vehicle and exiting the car park, the individual is being monitored in some capacity. To some or possibly many this is an invasion of privacy;

to others, this is a slight inconvenience for the added safety that is afforded their vehicle by the presence of the cameras. It is also noteworthy that most of the studies (four out of six) did not measure either displacement of crime or diffusion of benefits. On balance, the crime reduction benefits of the use of CCTV in car parks seem to outweigh any social costs.

CCTV in other public settings, such as city and town centers, public housing communities, and transportation facilities, evokes more resistance on the basis of threats to privacy and other civil liberties and are associated with a larger number of social harms, including the reinforcement of the notion of a fortress society and the social exclusion of marginalized populations (Clarke, 2000). Indeed, it is often these settings that are at the center of the debate over how best to strike a balance between the potential crime reduction benefits and social costs associated with CCTV (Savage, 2007).

Take city and town centers, for example. Here, the coverage of the cameras is much less than in car parks, but there is often a greater number of cameras extending over a larger area. For instance, a person walking down a street in an urban center could be caught on camera 20, 30, or 40 times, depending on the concentration of cameras. In London and other major cities in the United Kingdom, this concentration as well as its widespread use in other public (and private) places figured into the estimate that the average Briton is caught on camera roughly 300 times a day (Associated Press, 2007). CCTV in this setting may also result in the social exclusion of vulnerable or marginalized populations, such as unemployed youths who are hanging out and the homeless. The fear is that instead of providing assistance for these groups to get off the street (so to speak), CCTV, among other interventions like police and security guard patrols, may push them further away from available services and cause increased harm in the form of crime, victimization, or both. On the matter of crime displacement, it was most common to find evidence of no displacement.

Our finding that CCTV is associated with a nonsignificant and rather small 7% reduction in crimes in city and town centers does not detract from the need to assess its potential social harms. This is because city and town centers remain the most popular public setting for the implementation of this form of surveillance (Savage, 2007). So the main questions that confront policy makers over the use of CCTV in this public setting seem to be: How can its effectiveness be improved? How can CCTV be less intrusive? Both questions are important but difficult to answer.

From our meta-analysis of evaluations of CCTV in city and town centers, there is no clear indication about what may work best in this setting. However, lessons can be drawn from the effectiveness of CCTV in car parks. All six car park schemes included other interventions (e.g., improved lighting, security guards), were mostly limited to a reduction in vehicle crimes (the only crime type measured in five of the six schemes), and camera coverage was high for those evaluations that reported on it. In contrast, the evaluations of city and town center schemes measured a much larger range of crime types and only a small number of studies involved other interventions. (Too few studies reported on camera coverage.) This was also the case in public housing communities, in which we also found that CCTV was associated with a nonsignificant 7% reduction in crimes.

These findings point to the need for CCTV in city and town centers to be targeted on property crimes, targeted at specific places such as high-crime areas (as part of an effort to increase camera coverage), and combined with other surveillance measures. Regular crime analysis by the police, such as that used in CompStat, could be used to identify those places that are at greatest risk for property crimes, which, in turn, could be used to guide the implementation of video surveillance. The advent of mobile and redeployable CCTV cameras may make this a more feasible and perhaps less costly option (Waples and Gill, 2006). (In chapter 9, we discuss these and other new and emerging surveillance technologies.) This more targeted approach could also go some way toward reducing the pervasiveness of the threat to the general public's privacy and other civil liberties. Efforts to reduce any social exclusion effect associated with CCTV in this setting would need to involve other services.

Incidentally, we did not find any evidence that supports an association between the effectiveness of CCTV and those public places in which there is less resistance to its use, for example, in car parks. In chapter 5, we discussed the possibility that a contributing factor to the difference in effectiveness between the British CCTV schemes and those in other countries may have something to do with the public in other countries being less accepting and more apprehensive of CCTV. However, this view may be changing in the United States.

In public housing communities, the stakes are even higher in an effort to balance crime reduction and social costs. This is because people live there. What we do not know is whether residents of public housing communities are more or less supportive of CCTV than those who come in contact with it in other public settings. One view is that residents, who often do not have a say in its implementation, are distrustful of how CCTV will be used by the police or security company, not to mention the threat it presents to privacy. Another view is that residents are grateful for the added measure of security.

Similar to city and town centers, CCTV in public housing may be more effective and less intrusive if it is implemented in specific places where crime is more likely to take place. These hot spots could include the car park, playground, or park. As well, CCTV may be more effective if implemented in high-use areas, such as the main lobby, other points of entry or exit, elevators, and stairwells. Importantly, of the five schemes that measured displacement or diffusion, all of them reported that displacement did not occur.

The effects of CCTV on crime in public transportation facilities, specifically, underground railway systems or subways, raise other considerations. In our meta-analysis of the four evaluations of CCTV in this public setting, we found that it led to a sizable (23%) but nonsignificant reduction in crime. A substantial reduction in robberies and thefts in the first London Underground evaluation (an overall 61% decrease), conducted by John Burrows (1980), was the main reason for this large average effect size over all four studies. Only two studies measured displacement or diffusion, with one showing evidence of diffusion and the other showing evidence of displacement.

It is not altogether clear how CCTV could be more effective in this setting. Camera coverage was not reported in any of the evaluations; three of the four included other situational prevention measures (e.g., CCTV notices, passenger alarms) or in one case improved lighting; as already noted, crime reduction benefits accrued from a range of crimes, meaning that targeting property crimes alone may not be an effective strategy in this setting. On the matter of CCTV being less intrusive in subways, its use could be limited to those stations or lines that have the highest crime rates.

Like CCTV, the use of security guards in public places has also been criticized on the grounds that it may result in the social exclusion of vulnerable populations, such as unemployed youths and the homeless (Wakefield, 2003). The potential threat to privacy or other civil liberties associated with the presence of security guards may be somewhat less of a concern to the general public. Although no research has investigated this question, one of the possible reasons for this could be that unlike CCTV, this technique of formal surveillance is not as invasive; it does not monitor (and record) every move one makes.

Our finding that security guards represent a promising public area surveillance technique when implemented in car parks and targeted at vehicle crimes has some limitations in an analysis of crime reduction and social costs. This is because, as discussed in chapter 7, the promising nature of security guards means that we are not recommending their wider use but rather calling for additional evaluation research to test their effects under different conditions. Policy makers and practitioners should move cautiously. It is interesting that both techniques of formal surveillance—CCTV and security guards—share some of the same features with respect to the conditions under which they are deemed effective or promising: implemented in car parks, targeted at vehicle crimes, and combined with other measures. On this basis, too, further experimentation of the effectiveness of security guards seems warranted.

Improved street lighting—by far the most effective surveillance technique in reducing crime in public space—has some advantages over other surveillance measures that have been associated with the creeping privatization of public space, the exclusion of sections of the population, and the move toward a "fortress" society (Bottoms, 1990). Street lighting benefits the whole neighborhood rather than particular individuals or households. It has no adverse civil liberties implications, and it can increase public safety and effective use of neighborhood streets at night. It is also the case that improved street lighting does not displace crime. Only 3 of the 13 studies reported some or possible evidence that lighting improvements caused crime to be displaced to the surrounding areas. Nine other studies reported no evidence of territorial displacement, with two of these also reporting at least some evidence of diffusion of crime prevention benefits to nearby areas that did not receive the intervention.

The one potential social harm associated with street lighting is that it may contribute to light pollution (Pease, 1999). We do not deny that improved street lighting may cause an increase in light pollution, and this potential social cost should be considered in decisions to implement lighting schemes. However, for many, especially those who live in urban areas, this may be a small price to pay for the crime reduction benefits that have been shown to accrue from lighting improvements.

Like improved street lighting, the natural surveillance technique of defensible space may have few (if any) social costs. Defensible space involves design changes to the built environment to maximize the natural surveillance of open spaces afforded by people going about their day-to-day activities. It does not appear to violate personal privacy, infringe on civil liberties, or contribute to the social exclusion of groups. Conceivably some of the more structural design changes (e.g., construction of street barricades or closures, redesign of walkways, installation of windows) could evoke more resistance than some of the more mundane changes (e.g., removal or pruning of bushes in front of homes, removal of objects from store shelves or windows).

Our systematic review of defensible space found that the practice of street closures or barricades is effective in reducing crime in inner-city neighborhoods. Unfortunately, only two of the four studies reported on displacement or diffusion. In one case, there was some evidence of both displacement and diffusion, and in the other displacement did not occur. On balance, the crime reduction benefits of street barricades or closures in inner-city neighborhoods appear to outweigh any potential social costs.

Finally, we consider place managers. Our conclusion is that this surveillance technique is of unknown effectiveness in preventing crime in public places. Even so, it seems worthwhile to sketch out a rough crime reduction–social cost analysis.

Some may express concern with parking lot attendants, bus drivers, concierges, and other place managers as yet another set of eyes watching potential offenders and law-abiding citizens alike. Unlike security guards or CCTV, surveillance is a secondary function of place managers. This secondary function comes about from their presence and ability to intervene, thus presenting a deterrent threat to potential offenders. In this regard, the use of this surveillance technique may strike a fairly good balance between the public's interest in community safety and concerns over the erosion of privacy and civil liberties. More research is needed to investigate the effects of place managers on crime in public places.

Implications for Other Western Countries

In most of our systematic reviews of the different forms of public area surveillance, studies were included from a range of Western countries.

This often allowed for an analysis of differential effects between countries, notably the United States and Great Britain. For example, in the improved street lighting review, the included studies were carried out in one of these two countries. Results of the meta-analysis showed that street lighting improvements were much more effective in reducing crime in the United Kingdom than in the United States. In the CCTV review, a larger number of countries were represented in the included studies (Canada, Norway, Sweden, United Kingdom, and the United States). The best country comparison was between the United Kingdom and other countries. Results of the meta-analysis showed that CCTV was much more effective in reducing crime in the United Kingdom than in other countries.

So far our discussion has focused largely on the policy implications of these results for the United States. That is, from these international comparisons, our interest has been on the lessons that can be drawn from other countries to help improve the crime prevention effectiveness of public area surveillance in the United States. Here we take a look at what some of the key results mean for other Western countries.

The combination of CCTV with other surveillance (e.g., improved lighting, security guards) or situational or social (e.g., fencing, youth inclusion projects) measures seems to be an important contributing factor to the effectiveness of the British studies. Half of the 36 British schemes used one or more other types of interventions alongside CCTV, whereas not one of the eight schemes from the other countries (five of them from the United States) used other interventions. The implication here is that CCTV on its own may not represent a sufficient deterrent threat to influence an offender's decision-making process to commit a crime, and this seems to have been registered in the United Kingdom. No difference was found between the British and American improved street lighting schemes on their use of other interventions.

Cultural context is another important issue that may be a contributing factor to the difference in effectiveness between the British CCTV schemes and those in other countries. In the United Kingdom, there is a high level of public support for the use of CCTV cameras to prevent crime in public settings (Gill and Spriggs, 2005; Norris and Armstrong, 1999; Phillips, 1999). As noted, in the United States, at least during the period of time that the American CCTV schemes were implemented (before 2000), the public was less accepting and more apprehensive of Big Brother implications of the use of video surveillance in public places (Murphy, 2002; Rosen, 2004).

The overall poor showing of CCTV schemes in other countries, especially in the United States, could be due in part to this lack of public support and quite possibly a lack of political support. This may have resulted in cuts in program funding or the police assigning lower priority to the schemes, for example. Each of these factors could potentially undermine the effectiveness of CCTV schemes. That there have been only five high-quality evaluations of CCTV schemes in the United States so far may say something about this lack of public and political support for the use of video surveillance to reduce crime in public places. In the United Kingdom, then, it would seem that maintaining public and political support for CCTV may be important to its effectiveness.

Although cultural context could play a role in the differential effectiveness of street lighting in the two countries (to our knowledge there have been no recent surveys of the public in either country), we believe this is not likely. This is mainly because this form of surveillance is viewed as having few (if any) perceived harmful social consequences.

There may also be something of an age effect that contributed to the difference in effectiveness between the British and American street lighting studies. With the exception of one of the eight U.S. street lighting evaluations, all of them were carried out at least 10–15 years earlier than the first U.K. street lighting evaluation. Could it be that the U.K. evaluations drew on the knowledge gleaned from the previous U.S. evaluations and the detailed review by James Tien and his colleagues (1979), and that this played some role in the effectiveness of the U.K. lighting schemes? This is possible, because there was a great awareness of this American research, which is evidenced in British-based reviews of the literature (Painter, 1996; Ramsay and Newton, 1991) and some of the British lighting studies included in our review.

Another factor that may have contributed to the difference in effectiveness between the American and British street lighting schemes is the possibility that the offenders during the 1990s (in the case of the British studies) may have been influenced by different factors compared with those over a decade ago. There may also be differences between British and American offenders.

Disappointingly, less can be said about implications for other Western countries arising from the results of the other forms of public area surveillance. This is largely owing to there being no possibility for between-country comparisons. Our finding that place managers are of unknown effectiveness in preventing crime is more relevant to the U.K. than the U.S. context. This is because the two included studies in our review took place in the United Kingdom. As already noted, the key implication here is that this technique of public area surveillance could benefit from further evaluation research. Our finding that security guards are promising when implemented in car parks and targeted at vehicle crimes is based on two studies from different countries. For security guards, even more so than for place managers,[2] the implication is that this technique of formal surveillance could benefit from further experimentation.

On the matter of the defensible space practice of street closures or barricades, which we found to be effective in reducing crime when implemented in inner-city neighborhoods, all four studies included in our review took place in the United States. Although there was no possibility for an international comparison of the effects on crime, other countries could draw lessons from the U.S. experience with this natural surveillance technique. For example, as noted, the potential social costs associated with street closures or barricades are minimal if not nonexistent. These are particularly effective in high-crime areas and with a range of crimes. In three of the four studies, they were implemented in high-crime inner-city neighborhoods (the other case involved implementation across the city). Each study produced desirable effects on overall crime or on a specific crime type (violence in one case and property in another). One other important point that may have salience for other cities across the United States or in other countries is that the effectiveness of street closures or barricades is very much viewed as a product of increased natural surveillance on the part of residents who now feel safer being outside their homes—for example, walking the streets or visiting the park.

Surveillance in Private Space

This book is purposely focused on surveillance in public places. As discussed in chapter 1, this is not to deny the importance as well as the widespread use of surveillance measures to prevent crime in private domains. Instead, our specific focus on public places allows for a more comprehensive examination of one aspect of the current debate on surveillance and crime prevention. This focus also recognizes the growing use of surveillance measures to prevent crime in public places in the United States and in other Western nations.

Each public area surveillance measure discussed in this book is also used to prevent crime in private places. For example, the first use of CCTV cameras to prevent crime took place in the private sector. In the United Kingdom, cameras were first introduced in the retail sector; in the United States, it was in banking. It is common nowadays to encounter video surveillance in a wide range of private domains, including convenience stores, shopping malls, gas stations, banks, and even homes. Security guards are more often associated with the protection of private places,[3] but they are increasingly being used to protect public places (Sklansky, 2006).

Our specific focus on public area surveillance is the reason we did not assess the effects on crime of neighborhood watch programs. This highly popular form of citizen surveillance is most often used to prevent crimes at private residences. In a systematic review and meta-analysis of neighborhood watch, British criminologists Trevor Bennett, Katy Holloway, and David Farrington (2006) found this program to be effective in preventing crime.

There is still another dimension to our specific focus on public area surveillance. This pertains to the poor state of evaluation research on private area surveillance practices. We found few high-quality studies that evaluated the effects of surveillance measures on crime in private places. One of the reasons for this paucity of research is the private sector's resistance to independent evaluation of their practices and, equally important, making any evaluations (independent or otherwise) publicly available. Although there are some excellent evaluations of the application of situational crime prevention practices in the private sector (see e.g., Eck, 2006; Hunter and Jeffrey, 1997), until such time that the private sector embraces evaluation research more fully it will be difficult to assess in any comprehensive way the effectiveness of surveillance practices in preventing crime in private places. Another reason for the poor state of evaluation research in the private sector may stem from biases of criminologists about what is interesting and useful research and the fact that governments have not fully understood that assisting private security benefits the public sector as much as the private.

Conclusions

For some Americans, the idea of surveillance technology being used in public areas conjures up images of Orwell's Big Brother society—a society that is constantly watching (and recording) every move, every action that one takes (Stanley and Steinhardt, 2003). To return to a point made throughout this book, not all forms of surveillance are as potentially intrusive and raise questions about the infringement of civil liberties and other social costs. Importantly, these social costs need to be weighed against any crime prevention benefits that accrue from the different forms of surveillance.

The public area surveillance measures that we found to be effective in preventing crime seem to present few (if any) social costs to the general public. Improved street lighting is perhaps the most obvious. It is the most effective of the main surveillance techniques in preventing crime, and its only drawback is that it may cause an increase in light pollution. The defensible space practice of street closures or barricades in inner-city neighborhoods is also highly effective in preventing crime (both property and violent). By all accounts, it also does not appear to cause any undue hardship to residents in these areas. The only effective use of CCTV—when implemented in car parks and targeted at vehicle crimes—may cause little resistance on the part of the general citizenry, at least compared to its use in other public settings. Indeed, this is where the debate heats up. On one hand, CCTV is shown to be not very effective in preventing crime in city and town centers, public housing communities, and transportation facilities. On the other hand, in these areas the potential social costs are most troubling.

We do not anticipate that the use of CCTV will cease anytime soon in these other public areas, nor should it. What we do hope is that consideration is given to the research evidence on other public area surveillance measures that are effective (often in combination with other surveillance interventions), and that lessons from the effective use of CCTV may be applied to other conditions and contexts. Importantly, drawing on the lessons from the effective use of CCTV may not only go some way toward improving its crime prevention effectiveness in other public settings, it may also contribute to reducing its social costs. In this respect, results of between-country comparisons may also have some relevance for other Western countries.

In the next chapter, we offer some concluding thoughts and identify future directions to help make public places safer in this age of surveillance.

Conclusions and Future Directions

9

In his compelling book, *The Naked Crowd: Reclaiming Security and Freedom in an Anxious Age*, George Washington University legal scholar Jeffrey Rosen (2004) lucidly argues that it is feasible to strike a balance between improved security and the protection of civil liberties. The exponential growth of surveillance technology in all its varieties, from closed-circuit television (CCTV) cameras in city centers to enhanced passenger screening at airports, in the wake of the terrorist attacks on the United States on September 11, 2001, does not necessarily have to coincide with a concomitant reduction in the protection of civil liberties. Instead, there is much that can be done to improve surveillance technologies, and Rosen explores these possibilities.

The improved technology thesis is highly relevant to this book's focus on surveillance and crime prevention in public places. Two connected lines of thought seem most important. One is that there are other forms of surveillance that may be equally or more effective in reducing crime in public places. This is in contrast to the current narrow focus on CCTV in the United States and in some other Western countries. The second point is that these other public area surveillance measures may impose fewer social costs on society. As we discussed in chapter 8, the latter is sometimes more difficult to gauge, but it is an important consideration in the debate on the use of surveillance in public places. Broadening the view of public area surveillance for crime prevention was a key aim of this book.

Another key goal was to advance evidence-led policy in this area. This involved adopting an evidence-based framework to assess what works best. It meant using only the highest quality evaluation research and the most rigorous methods to identify, collect, and analyze the accumulated evidence. Importantly, this approach ensures that our conclusions are based on the best available research.

Other Potential Benefits

One of the issues that this book was not able to explore was that public area surveillance might produce other important benefits beyond a reduction in crime rates. Many of the surveillance measures examined herein also serve other purposes in public places. To our knowledge, few of these other uses have been the subject of high-quality evaluations. Indeed, our reporting of program effects on crime—over and above our focus on surveillance and crime prevention—was driven largely by what high-quality evaluations have measured.

Improvements in street lighting may also provide benefits (during the nighttime hours) in the form of, for example, increased pedestrian and traffic safety and increased usage of public parks and other recreational areas. Previous reviews of the literature report mixed results on the effects of street lighting on road traffic injuries (Beyer, Pond, and Ker, 2005). Street lighting, as well as the other forms of public area surveillance, may also foster private enterprise. The increased pedestrian traffic that can flow from street lighting might also translate into increased patronage for businesses in the area.

In the case of the other natural surveillance technique of defensible space, the implementation of street barricades or closures in (mostly high-crime) inner-city neighborhoods led to increased usage of streets, parks, and other public places by the residents. This is an important benefit by itself. The authors of the studies argued that this mechanism of natural surveillance influenced the reduction in crime. Improvements in residents' perceptions of crime provided support for this position. Increased pedestrian and traffic safety may be another benefit of street closures or barricades.

There seem to be many more potential benefits associated with CCTV. For the police, the potential benefit of CCTV in reducing crime by deterring offenders from committing an illegal activity may be lower on its list of priorities than the apprehension of suspects who were caught on camera committing a crime (see Norris and McCahill, 2006). The use of a camera image to aid in the identification and apprehension of a suspect, as well as help secure a conviction in criminal court, is a common justification that is used by police and prosecutors alike in many U.S. cities that are currently experimenting with increased use of video surveillance in public places (Ballou, 2007; McCarthy, 2007).

Police officer safety is another potential benefit associated with CCTV. This has come about through the installation of CCTV cameras in patrol cars to record the events of roadside stops, for example. The use of CCTV in city and town centers and other public places could also potentially contribute to improved police officer safety. Like the other forms of surveillance, CCTV could result in increased pedestrian and traffic safety. This could follow from the use of speed cameras and traffic light cameras (i.e., to record vehicles going through red lights at intersections), which are already used extensively in some cities in the United States and elsewhere.

To return to a point raised in chapter 3, innovative policing strategies like problem-oriented policing (POP) often incorporate situational crime prevention measures of a surveillance or nonsurveillance nature. In this regard, police operations may benefit from the use of CCTV and other public area surveillance measures. At least with respect to CCTV, its use in combination with other crime prevention measures and targeted on a specific crime (a feature of POP) may make it an effective component of some POP initiatives. However, this may not necessarily be the case with respect to more traditional policing practices. In a study of the impact of public area CCTV on policing in the southern region of England, Oxford criminologist Benjamin Goold (2004, p. 212) found that "policing practices in the six towns included in this study did not change significantly as a result of the introduction of CCTV." He went on to add, "Cameras alone do not make the police more repressive or authoritarian, any more than they make the police more effective or efficient" (p. 212).

Another potential benefit associated with CCTV is the prevention of terrorist activities, whether through the identification of suspicious persons or packages that prevent the act from taking place or through the identification, apprehension, and conviction of suspects after the act.

Mainly this latter function of CCTV was used to justify its widespread implementation in both public and private places throughout Britain in the 1990s (Rosen, 2001) and, following the suicide bombings on the London Underground in July 2005, reaffirm its utility there (Hier, Walby, and Greenberg, 2006).

Similarly, in the United States, the terrorist acts perpetrated on September 11, 2001, have contributed to an increased use of CCTV surveillance cameras in this country (Clymer, 2002; Murphy, 2002). Much of the funding for this expansion has come in the form of grants to cities from the U.S. Department of Homeland Security. The amount that has been spent so far on cameras is unknown, but an analysis conducted by the *Boston Globe* estimates that "a large number of new surveillance systems, costing at least tens and probably hundreds of millions of dollars, are being simultaneously installed around the country as part of homeland security grants" (Savage, 2007). In some cities, like New York, combating terrorism is seemingly the top priority (Associated Press, 2006b). In other cities, like Boston and Los Angeles, cameras have also been implemented in areas faced with increased problems of gang violence, drug dealing, and other street crimes (Ballou, 2007; Winton, 2006).

Security guards and place managers could also play a role in preventing terrorist acts. It has been suggested that security guards are the first line of defense in this age of terrorism (Joh, 2004, p. 49). In the case of place managers, the surveillance function is secondary to their day-to-day employment duties as parking lot attendants, train conductors, and so on. The value that society places on these roles could be considered as other potential benefits.

Research Priorities

Advancing knowledge about the effectiveness of the different forms of surveillance for making public places safer from crime should begin with attention to the methodological rigor of the evaluation designs. The minimum acceptable evaluation design is to have before-and-after measures of crime in experimental and comparable control areas. It is desirable in future evaluations to compare several experimental areas with several comparable control areas. If the areas were relatively small, it might be possible to randomly allocate them to experimental and control conditions or to have alternate periods with or without surveillance. In addition, future evaluations should include interviews with potential offenders and potential victims to find out what they know about the surveillance scheme and their views on associated social costs, test hypotheses about mediators between the surveillance measure and crime, and have measures of crime other than those from official sources (Farrington and Painter, 2003).

It would be desirable to have a long time series of crime rates in experimental and comparable control areas before and after an intervention to investigate regression to the mean (which happens if an intervention is implemented just after an unusually high crime rate period) as well as the persistence of any effects on crime. In the situational crime prevention literature, brief follow-up periods are the norm, but "it is now recognized that more information is needed about the longer-term effects of situational prevention" (Clarke, 2001, p. 29). Ideally, the same time periods should be used in before-and-after measures of crime. Also, it is important to disentangle the effects of CCTV, for example, from the effects of other interventions, such as improved street lighting or security guards. For example, an experiment could include four conditions in a Latin square design: CCTV plus improved lighting, CCTV alone, improved lighting alone, and neither.

In planning an evaluation, it is important to ensure that there is sufficient statistical power to detect any effect of the surveillance measure on crime. In other words, the number of crimes in each condition before the intervention should be substantial. Also, effects should be measured for different types of crimes. Displacement of crime and diffusion of crime prevention benefits should be studied by comparing experimental areas with adjacent and nonadjacent control areas. If crime decreased in an experimental area, increased in an adjacent control area, and stayed constant in a nonadjacent control area, this might be evidence of displacement. If crime decreased in an experimental area and in an adjacent control area but stayed constant or increased in a nonadjacent control area, this might be evidence of diffusion of benefits.

Hypotheses about moderators should be tested by classifying types of areas and types of people living in them and seeing how these factors are related to the effects of surveillance measures on crime. It is important to monitor changes in the surveillance measures over time and any implementation problems, as well as changes in other factors in the areas that might influence crime. In the case of CCTV, for example, the intensity of its coverage and other features of these schemes (e.g., the probability of police or security responding to incidents seen on CCTV) should be assessed to investigate if there is a dose-response relationship between these features and the effect size. Any publicity about the surveillance scheme should be documented.

The effect size, confidence intervals, and statistical significance should be calculated. The most meaningful effect size measure is the change in crime in an experimental area compared with a control area. In studying the effect on crime of a surveillance measure, regression analyses can be carried out that control for prior crimes and for individual and community factors that influence crime. Cost-benefit analyses should be conducted to assess whether the financial benefits of the surveillance measure outweighs its monetary costs. It is also important to conduct cost-effectiveness analyses to assess how the surveillance measure compares with other alternatives in the cost of reducing crimes. It would be desirable to broaden the scope of evaluations of public area surveillance schemes to include other important outcomes, such as pedestrian and traffic safety. This could be achieved through collaborations with researchers in other academic disciplines. Ideally, the evaluators of the schemes should be independent of the implementers and funders and should have no stake in the outcome of the evaluation. At a minimum, any possible conflict of interest should be declared.

Advancing knowledge about the effectiveness of the different forms of surveillance could also benefit from testing the main theories (i.e., situational crime prevention versus community investment) more explicitly. Surveys of youth in experimental and control areas could be carried out to investigate their offending, their opinions of the area, their street use patterns, and factors that might inhibit them from offending (e.g., informal social control by older residents, increased surveillance after dark). Household surveys of adults could also be carried out, focusing on perceptions of improvements in the community, community pride, informal social control of young people, street use, and surveillance after dark. Systematic observations of areas would also be useful.

Emerging Developments

Of the major forms of surveillance covered in this book, CCTV more than any other is subject to profound changes in its implementation and use in public places in the years ahead. Already, we have cataloged many of

CCTV's other potential benefits beyond a reduction in crime rates. Perhaps most dramatic on the matter of emerging developments are changes in its technology. These include (but are not limited to) facial recognition applications; digital monitoring and storage capabilities; covert, mobile, and redeployable cameras; and camera networks that allow for the tracking of offenders (Nieto, Johnston-Dodds, and Simmons, 2002; Surette, 2005). These technological advancements have radically changed the debate over the need for legal controls and regulations governing the use of CCTV in public places (Marx, 2005; Nieto, Johnston-Dodds, and Simmons, 2002; Williams and Johnstone, 2000).

We found that CCTV is effective when implemented in car parks and targeted at vehicle crimes. An analysis of social costs suggests that there may be little resistance to the use of CCTV in this setting. This may change with the advent of more technologically sophisticated systems, and may have further ramifications in other public settings where CCTV is not very effective in reducing crime and may impose more social costs on the law-abiding citizenry (i.e., city and town centers, public housing communities, and public transportation systems). Whatever technological changes are introduced, policy makers and practitioners need to strive for the most effective and socially noninvasive use of CCTV in public places.

Technology may also play a role with respect to the natural surveillance technique of improved street lighting, albeit far less so than CCTV. We found that improved street lighting was by far the most effective public area surveillance technique. Just as lighting levels and styles are important to crime prevention effectiveness, technological improvements in lighting may reduce the one social cost associated with its use: light pollution.

Less can be said about emerging developments with respect to the defensible space practice of street closures or barricades (another technique of natural surveillance) and place managers. We found that street closures or barricades are effective in preventing crime in inner-city neighborhoods, whereas place managers appear to be of unknown effectiveness in preventing crime in public places. In both cases, an analysis of social costs suggests that there may be little or no resistance on the part of the public. There seems to be ample room for experimentation with the use of place managers in public places. This is related to the fact that surveillance is a secondary function of place managers. In this regard, place managers may strike a fairly good balance between crime reduction and social costs.

With respect to the formal surveillance technique of security guards, one noteworthy development is their growing use in public places (Sklansky, 2006). It is unclear at this time if this represents a positive development for crime reduction. It may be more related to the changing balance between private and public policing (Sklansky, 2008).

From our review of the research evidence, we found that security guards represent a promising public area surveillance technique when implemented in car parks and targeted at vehicle crimes. At least compared to its formal surveillance counterpart in CCTV, the potential threat to privacy or other civil liberties may be less of a concern to the general public. To be clear, we are not recommending the wider use of security guards but calling for additional evaluation research to test their effects under different conditions.

Last, there is some evidence of the effectiveness of combining the different forms of public area surveillance. Perhaps it is time for policy makers, practitioners, and researchers to look more closely at how to maximize their shared effectiveness in reducing crime and capitalize on their different qualities. This seems to be particularly important in an effort to strive for the most effective and socially noninvasive use of surveillance to make public places safer from crime.

Appendix

Methods of Systematic Review and Meta-Analysis

Systematic Review

This book reports on systematic reviews of the effects on crime of the five major forms of public area surveillance: closed-circuit television (CCTV), improved street lighting, security guards, place managers, and defensible space.

Criteria for Inclusion of Evaluation Studies

In selecting evaluations for inclusion in each of the five systematic reviews, the following criteria were used.

a. The surveillance measure in question was the main focus of the intervention. For evaluations involving one or more interventions, only those in which the surveillance measure in question was the main intervention were included. The determination of the main intervention was based on the author identifying it as such or, if the author did not do this, the importance the report gave the primary intervention compared to any other interventions.

b. There was an outcome measure of crime. The most relevant crime outcomes were violent and property crimes (including vehicle crimes).
c. The evaluation design was of high methodological quality, with the minimum design involving before-and-after measures of crime in experimental and comparable control areas. In a few of the included studies, the comparability of the experimental and control areas was difficult to gauge or not as strong as the others. We were reluctant to exclude these studies unless they were clearly inadequate.
d. The total number of crimes in each area before the intervention was at least 20. The main measure of effect size was based on changes in numbers of crimes between the before-and-after time periods. It was considered that a measure of change based on an N below 20 was potentially misleading. Also, any study with fewer than 20 crimes before would have insufficient statistical power to detect changes in crime. The criterion of 20 is probably too low, but we were reluctant to exclude studies unless their numbers were clearly inadequate.

Search Strategies

To locate studies meeting the above criteria, four search strategies were employed:

a. Searches of electronic bibliographic databases.
b. Searches of reviews of the literature on the effects on crime of the surveillance measure in question.
c. Searches of bibliographies of evaluation reports of applicable studies.
d. Contacts with leading researchers.

Both published and unpublished reports were considered in these searches. Furthermore, the searches were international in scope and were not limited to the English language.

CCTV

The following terms were used to search the databases for CCTV evaluations: closed circuit television, CCTV, cameras, social control, surveillance, and formal surveillance. When applicable, "crime" was then added to each of these terms (e.g., CCTV and crime) to narrow the search parameters.

The search strategies (over two periods of time) resulted in the collection of a total of 44 evaluations of CCTV that met the inclusion criteria. Forty-eight other evaluations were obtained and analyzed but did not meet the inclusion criteria and were excluded. The majority of these evaluations were excluded because they did not use a control area. (This was also the case in the other reviews.) Two other evaluation reports were identified, but we were not successful in obtaining copies. Information on the excluded and unobtainable evaluations (for all five reviews) is available from the first author.

Improved Street Lighting

The following terms were used to search the databases for street lighting evaluations: street lighting, lighting, illumination, and natural surveillance. When applicable, "crime" was then added to each of these terms (e.g., street lighting and crime) to narrow the search parameters.

The search strategies (also over two periods of time) resulted in the collection of a total of 13 evaluations of improved street lighting that met the inclusion criteria. Twenty other evaluations were obtained and analyzed but did not meet the inclusion criteria and were excluded. Four other evaluation reports were identified, but we were not successful in obtaining copies.

Security Guards

The following terms were used to search the databases for security guard evaluations: security guards, private police, formal surveillance, and guardian. When applicable, "crime," "surveillance," "systematic review," and "effectiveness" were added to each of these terms (e.g., security guards and crime) to narrow the search parameters.

The search strategies resulted in the collection of a total of five evaluations of security guards that met the inclusion criteria. Four other evaluations were obtained and analyzed but did not meet the inclusion criteria and were excluded.

Place Managers

The following terms were used to search the databases for place manager evaluations: employee, place manager, guardian, conductor, attendant, park keeper, doorman, assistant, and occupational presence. When applicable, "crime," "surveillance," "supervision," and "effectiveness" were then added to each of these terms (e.g., place managers and crime) to narrow the search parameters.

The search strategies resulted in the collection of only two evaluations of place managers that met the inclusion criteria. Five other evaluations were obtained and analyzed but did not meet the inclusion criteria and were excluded.

Defensible Space

The following terms were used to search the databases for defensible space evaluations: defensible space and CPTED (crime prevention through environmental design). When applicable, "crime," "surveillance," "road closures," "barricades," and "prevention" were then added to each of these terms (e.g., defensible space and crime) to narrow the search parameters. "Defensible space" and "CPTED" were also used together along with these other terms to narrow the search parameters.

The search strategies resulted in the collection of a total of five evaluations of defensible space that met the inclusion criteria. Four other evaluations were obtained and analyzed but did not meet the inclusion criteria and were excluded.

Meta-Analysis

To carry out a meta-analysis, a comparable measure of effect size and an estimate of its variance are needed in each program evaluation (Lipsey and Wilson, 2001; Wilson, 2001). In the case of both CCTV and street lighting evaluations, the measure of effect size had to be based on the number of crimes in the experimental and control areas before and after the intervention. This is because this was the only information that was regularly provided in these evaluations. Here, the odds ratio (OR) is used as the measure of effect size. For example, in the Doncaster city center CCTV evaluation by David Skinns (1998), the odds of a crime after given a crime before in the control area were 2,002/1,780 or 1.12. The odds of a crime after given a crime before in the experimental area were 4,591/5,832 or 0.79. The OR, therefore, was 1.12/0.79 or 1.42.

The OR has a very simple and meaningful interpretation. It indicates the proportional change in crime in the control area compared with the experimental area. In this example, the OR of 1.42 indicates that crime increased by 42% in the control area compared with the experimental area. An OR of 1.42 could also indicate that crime decreased by 30% in the experimental area compared with the control area, because the change in the experimental area compared with the control area is the inverse of the OR, or 1/1.42 (0.70) here. The OR is calculated from the following table.

	Before	After
Experimental	a	b
Control	c	d

Here, a, b, c, and d are numbers of crimes:

$$OR = a*d/b*c.$$

The variance of OR is calculated from the variance of LOR (the natural logarithm of OR). The usual calculation of this is as follows:

$$V(LOR) = 1/a + 1/b + 1/c + 1/d.$$

To produce a summary effect size in a meta-analysis, each effect size is weighted according to the inverse of the variance. This was another reason for choosing the OR, which has a known variance (Fleiss, 1981, pp. 61–67).

The estimate of the variance is based on the assumption that total numbers of crimes (a, b, c, d) have a Poisson distribution. Thirty years of mathematical models of criminal careers have been dominated by the assumption that crimes can be accurately modeled by a Poisson process (Piquero, Farrington, and Blumstein, 2003). However, the large number of changing extraneous factors that influence the number of crimes may cause overdispersion; that is, where the variance of the number of crimes VAR exceeds the number of crimes N. The equation

$$D = VAR/N$$

specifies the overdispersion factor. Where there is overdispersion, V(LOR) should be multiplied by D. David Farrington, Martin Gill, Sam Waples, and Javier Argomaniz (2007) estimated VAR from monthly numbers of crimes and found the following equation:

$$D = .0008 * N + 1.2.$$

D increased linearly with N and was correlated .77 with N. The mean number of crimes in an area in the CCTV studies was about 760, suggesting that the mean value of D was about 2. For the lighting studies, the mean number of crimes in an area was about 445, suggesting that the mean value of D was about 1.6. However, for both cases this is an overestimate because the monthly variance is inflated by seasonal variations, which do not apply to N and VAR. Nevertheless, to obtain a conservative estimate, V(LOR) calculated from the usual formula was multiplied by D (estimated from the foregoing equation) in all cases. This adjustment corrects for overdispersion within studies but not for heterogeneity between studies. (For a more detailed discussion of the variance in the case of CCTV, see Farrington, Gill, Waples, and Argomaniz, 2007; for lighting, see Farrington and Welsh, 2004.)

Notes

Chapter 1

1. We did not find any high-quality evaluations of the effects on crime of surveillance measures in schools, universities, or government buildings.

Chapter 2

1. The earliest recorded use of public street lighting to aid in the reduction of crime dates back to 1667 in France during the reign of Louis XIV. In later years, the king placed the responsibility for lighting under the control of street police (Zahm, 2004, p. 536).

2. This percentage change is more accurately expressed as a reduction in crimes in experimental areas compared to comparable control areas.

3. This percentage change is more accurately expressed as a reduction in crimes in experimental areas compared to comparable control areas.

4. It is important to note that none of the sites in the national evaluation were included in our original systematic review.

5. Sklansky (2006, p. 92) confirms that this is the most recent accounting of the private security industry in the United States. He does not offer a reason for why there has not been a more recent study. We are left to speculate that this could be connected with the lack of public funding to pay for such a study. The *Hallcrest Report II*, by William Cunningham, John Strauchs, and Clifford Van Meter (1990), was funded by a grant from the National Institute of Justice.

Chapter 3

1. Ronald Clarke and Ross Homel (1997), in an earlier taxonomy of situational crime prevention, also identified three forms of surveillance: formal surveillance, informal surveillance, and surveillance by employees. In the most recent iteration by Cornish and Clarke (2003), the last form is renamed "place managers," but its meaning is not altered.

2. Per-Olof Wikström (1998) notes that the "classic" view of social disorganization theory is characterized more by the structural factors of low economic status, ethnic heterogeneity, and residential mobility (see also Sampson and Lauritsen, 1994).

3. For rebuttals of the Broken Windows hypothesis, see Harcourt (2001), Harcourt and Ludwig (2006), Sampson and Raudenbush (2001), and Taylor (2006).

Chapter 4

1. Descriptive validity, which refers to the adequacy of reporting of information, could be added as a fifth criterion of the methodological quality of evaluation research (Farrington, 2003; see also Lösel and Koferl, 1989).

2. *Statistical power* refers to the probability of correctly rejecting the null hypothesis (of no effect of the intervention) when it is false (i.e., when the intervention really has an effect on crime). Studies based on small numbers may not yield statistically significant results even when the intervention has a large effect on crime.

3. We estimated the importance of regression to the mean using recorded crime rates in police Basic Command Units in England and Wales in 2002–2003 and 2003–2004, and concluded that in reasonable comparisons between areas with high and moderately high crime rates, this effect may cause a 4% decrease in crimes (Farrington and Welsh, 2006b).

4. The key feature of randomized experiments is that the random assignment equates the experimental and control groups before the experimental intervention on all possible extraneous variables that might influence the outcome (e.g., crime). Hence, any subsequent differences between the groups must be attributable to the intervention. Randomization is the only method of assignment that controls for unknown and unmeasured confounders as well as those that are known and measured (Weisburd, Lum, and Petrosino, 2001). However, the randomized experiment is only the most convincing method of evaluation if it is implemented with full integrity. To the extent that there are implementation problems (e.g., problems of maintaining random assignment, differential attrition, crossover between control and experimental conditions), internal validity could be reduced.

5. Although not as rigorous as these two methods, another widely used and robust review method is vote counting. It adds a quantitative element to the

narrative review by counting the number of statistically significant and desirable findings out of all findings.

6. The criterion of methodological quality that is used for including (or excluding) studies is perhaps the "most important and controversial" issue in conducting systematic reviews (Farrington and Petrosino, 2001, p. 42). How high to set the bar of methodological rigor as part of a review of the literature, systematic or otherwise, is a question that all researchers face. For a brief discussion of this issue in the context of the vote-counting review method, see MacKenzie (2000).

7. It is beyond the scope of this chapter to discuss each step, but interested readers should consult the reviews of this methodology as applied in the context of situational and other forms of crime prevention (see Welsh and Farrington, 2000). In addition, for methodological features of cost-benefit analysis in general, see Layard and Glaister (1994) and Welsh, Farrington, and Sherman (2001).

8. Martha Smith, Ronald Clarke, and Ken Pease (2002) argue that researchers should also investigate the closely related phenomenon of "anticipatory benefits," whereby crime reduction benefits occur earlier than anticipated. The authors note that there are many possible reasons for this to occur, including publicity by project organizers or the media.

Chapter 5

1. Odds ratio effect sizes could not be calculated for three studies because numbers of crimes were not reported in the city/town center schemes in Ilford (Squires, 1998) or (for the control area) Sutton (Sarno, 1996) or for the public housing scheme in Brooklyn (Williamson and McLafferty, 2000).

2. In the evaluation of this program, any effect of the police patrols was controlled for by using as the before period the 12 months prior to the patrols coming into operation. The police patrols were discontinued at the time CCTV was implemented, so there was no direct influence of the patrols during the after period.

3. Fourteen of the 44 studies included in this review were part of this national evaluation of CCTV in Britain.

4. This is not one of the included (or excluded) CCTV studies. To our knowledge, no evaluation of CCTV in MacArthur Park has been conducted.

Chapter 6

1. In the interests of calculating a single effect size, the figures are combined in figure 6.1.

2. Our measure of effect size in Dudley was based on the victim survey because we considered that this yielded the most valid measure of crime.

3. Because the 13 effect sizes were significantly heterogeneous ($Q = 37.13$, 12 d.f., $p = 0.0002$), a random effects model was used here. Fixed effects models were

used when the heterogeneity was not significant. The fixed and random effects models, and the other models used by Jones (2005), all produced very similar weighted mean effect sizes.

4. The three studies that could not be included in this analysis were Indianapolis, Dover, and Birmingham. Indianapolis was not included because the areas were tiny (only two or three blocks); Dover because the area was a parking garage; and Birmingham because the area was a city center market.

Chapter 7

1. At the time, criminal incidents on the subway accounted for about 2.7% of all police-reported crime in New York City.

2. Australian criminologists Lorraine Mazerolle and Janet Ransley (2005) refer to place managers in the context of third-party policing. A search of the studies they included in their systematic review did not turn up any evaluations of place managers that involved surveillance for crime prevention in public space.

3. The sociodemographic profiles of the residents of the two high rises were very similar (Skilton, 1988).

4. Capital costs were not included on the costs side of the ledger because they need to be spread over time, usually over the scheme's expected life span, along with corresponding debt charges (Safe Neighbourhoods Unit, 1993, p. 145). A reasonable estimate of the program's life expectancy was unclear.

Chapter 8

1. Disappointingly, too few of the included studies carried out a cost-benefit analysis to allow for this important dimension to be considered here. We return to this subject in chapter 9.

2. This has to do with the formal meaning of *promising* (see chapter 7).

3. David Farrington and his colleagues (1993) conducted one of the few high-quality evaluations of the effects of security guards on crime in private space.

References

Armitage, Rachel. 2000. *An Evaluation of Secured by Design Housing within West Yorkshire*. Policing and Reducing Crime Unit Briefing Note. London: Home Office.

Armitage, Rachel. 2006. "Predicting and Preventing: Developing a Risk Assessment Mechanism for Residential Housing." *Crime Prevention and Community Safety*, 8(3): 137–149.

Armitage, Rachel. 2007. "Sustainability versus Safety: Confusion, Conflict and Contradictions in Designing out Crime." In *Imagination for Crime Prevention: Essays in Honour of Ken Pease. Crime Prevention Studies*, vol. 21, Graham Farrell, Kate J. Bowers, Shane D. Johnson, and Michael Townsley, eds. Monsey, N.Y.: Criminal Justice Press.

Armitage, Rachel, Graham Smyth, and Ken Pease. 1999. "Burnley CCTV Evaluation." In *Surveillance of Public Space: CCTV, Street Lighting and Crime Prevention. Crime Prevention Studies*, vol. 10, Kate Painter and Nick Tilley, eds. Monsey, N.Y.: Criminal Justice Press.

Associated Press. 2006a. "NYC to Put Cameras on Buses." *New York Times*, May 24, 2006. Available at www.nytimes.com.

Associated Press. 2006b. "NYPD Deploys First of 500 Cameras." *New York Times*, April 17, 2006. Available at www.nytimes.com.

Associated Press. 2007. "U.K. Privacy Watchdog Seeks More Powers." *New York Times*, May 2, 2007. Available at www.nytimes.com.

Associated Press. 2008. "Chicago Schools Add Cameras, Security Personnel." Available at www.wbbm780.com.

Athens Banner-Herald. 2008. "Editorial: Commission Due Credit for Acting on Principle." *Athens Banner-Herald*, September 3, 2008. Available at www.onlineathens.com.

Atkins, Stephen, Sohail Husain, and Angela Storey. 1991. *The Influence of Street Lighting on Crime and Fear of Crime*. Crime Prevention Unit Paper, no. 28. London: Home Office.

Atlanta Regional Commission. 1974. *Street Light Project: Final Evaluation Report*. Atlanta, Ga.: Atlanta Regional Commission.

Atlas, Randall, and William G. LeBlanc. 1994. "The Impact on Crime of Street Closures and Barricades: A Florida Case Study." *Security Journal* 5(3): 140–145.

Aued, Blake. 2008a. "Streetlight Cuts Stir Crime Fears." *Athens Banner-Herald*, July 17, 2008. Available at www.onlineathens.com.

Aued, Blake. 2008b. "Retreat on Light Cutoffs." *Athens Banner-Herald*, August 21, 2008. Available at www.onlineathens.com.

Ballou, Brian R. 2007. "Police to Widen Use of Cameras: Cite Aid Provided in 2 Homicide Cases." *Boston Globe*, September 23, 2007. Available at www.boston.com.

Barclay, Paul, Jennifer Buckley, Paul J. Brantingham, Patricia L. Brantingham, and Terry Whinn-Yates. 1996. "Preventing Auto Theft in Suburban Vancouver Commuter Lots: Effects of a Bike Patrol." In *Preventing Mass Transit Crime. Crime Prevention Studies*, vol. 6, Ronald V. Clarke, ed. Monsey, N.Y.: Criminal Justice Press.

Barnett, W. Steven. 1993. "Cost-Benefit Analysis." In *Significant Benefits: The High/Scope Perry Preschool Study through Age 27*, Lawrence J. Schweinhart, Helen V. Barnes, and David P. Weikart. Ypsilanti, Mich.: High/Scope Press.

Barr, Robert, and Ken Pease. 1990. "Crime Placement, Displacement, and Deflection". In *Crime and Justice: A Review of Research*, vol. 12, Michael Tonry and Norval Morris, eds. Chicago: University of Chicago Press.

Bennett, Trevor H. 1998. "Crime Prevention." In *The Handbook of Crime and Punishment*, Michael Tonry, ed. New York: Oxford University Press.

Bennett, Trevor H., Katy Holloway, and David P. Farrington. 2006. "Does Neighborhood Watch Reduce Crime? A Systematic Review and Meta-Analysis." *Journal of Experimental Criminology* 2: 437–458.

Bennett, Trevor H., and Richard Wright. 1984. *Burglars on Burglary*. Farnborough, Hants, U.K.: Gower.

Beyer, Fiona R., Philip Pond, and Katharine Ker. 2005. *Street Lighting for Preventing Road Traffic Injuries*. Cochrane Collaboration Protocol. Newcastle-upon-Tyne, U.K.: Centre for Health Services Research, University of Newcastle.

Blankstein, Andrew, and Ari B. Bloomekatz. 2008. "Police Cameras' View Fading; After Initial Success, a Lack of Maintenance on MacArthur Park Units May be Linked to a Rise in Serious Crimes." *Los Angeles Times*, January 16, 2008. Available at www.latimes.com.

Blixt, Madeleine. 2003. *The Use of Surveillance Cameras for the Purpose of Crime Prevention*. English Summary. Stockholm: National Council for Crime Prevention.

Blumstein, Alfred, Jacqueline Cohen, and Daniel S. Nagin, eds. 1978. *Deterrence and Incapacitation*. Washington, D.C.: National Academies Press.

Bottoms, Anthony E. 1990. "Crime Prevention Facing the 1990s." *Policing and Society* 1: 3–22.

Bottoms, Anthony, and James Dignan. 2004. "Youth Justice in Great Britain." In *Youth Crime and Youth Justice: Comparative and Cross-National Perspectives. Crime and Justice: A Review of Research*, vol. 31, Michael Tonry and Anthony N. Doob, eds. Chicago: University of Chicago Press.

Braga, Anthony A. 2006. "Policing Crime Hot Spots." In *Preventing Crime: What Works for Children, Offenders, Victims, and Places*, Brandon C. Welsh and David P. Farrington, eds. New York: Springer.

Braga, Anthony A. 2008. *Problem-Oriented Policing and Crime Prevention*, 2nd ed. Monsey, N.Y.: Criminal Justice Press.

Brown, Ben. 1995. *CCTV in Town Centres: Three Case Studies*. Crime Detection and Prevention Series Paper, no. 68. London: Home Office.

Burgess, Ernest W. 1942. "Introduction." In *Juvenile Delinquency and Urban Areas: A Study of Rates of Delinquents in Relation to Differential Characteristics of Local Communities in American Cities*, Clifford R. Shaw and Henry D. McKay. Chicago: University of Chicago Press.

Burrows, John N. 1980. "Closed Circuit Television on the London Underground." In *Designing out Crime*, Ronald V. Clarke and Patricia Mayhew, eds. London: Her Majesty's Stationery Office.

Bursik, Robert J., and Harold G. Grasmick. 1993. *Neighborhoods and Crime: The Dimensions of Effective Community Control*. New York: Lexington Books.

Campbell, Donald T. 1969. "Reforms as Experiments." *American Psychologist* 24: 409–429.

Campbell, Donald T., and Julian C. Stanley. 1966. *Experimental and Quasi-Experimental Designs for Research*. Chicago: Rand McNally.

Campbell, Duncan, and Sandra Laville. 2005. "British Suicide Bombers Carried out London Attacks, Say Police." *Guardian*, July 13, 2005. Available at www.guardian.co.uk.

Challinger, Dennis. 1992. "Less Telephone Vandalism: How Did It Happen?" In *Situational Crime Prevention: Successful Case Studies*, Ronald V. Clarke, ed. Albany, N.Y.: Harrow and Heston.

Chicago Tribune. 2008. "Editorial: Wave—and Behave." *Chicago Tribune,* February 10, 2008. Available at www.chicagotribune.com.

Clarke, Ronald V. 1992. "Introduction." In *Situational Crime Prevention: Successful Case Studies,* Ronald V. Clarke, ed. Albany, N.Y.: Harrow and Heston.

Clarke, Ronald V. 1995a. "Opportunity-Reducing Crime Prevention Strategies and the Role of Motivation." In *Integrating Crime Prevention Strategies: Propensity and Opportunity,* Per-Olof H. Wikström, Ronald V. Clarke, and Joan McCord, eds. Stockholm: National Council for Crime Prevention.

Clarke, Ronald V. 1995b. "Situational Crime Prevention." In *Building a Safer Society: Strategic Approaches to Crime Prevention. Crime and Justice: A Review of Research,* vol. 19, Michael Tonry and David P. Farrington, eds. Chicago: University of Chicago Press.

Clarke, Ronald V. 1997. "Introduction." In *Situational Crime Prevention: Successful Case Studies,* 2nd ed., Ronald V. Clarke, ed. Guilderland, N.Y.: Harrow and Heston.

Clarke, Ronald V. 2000. "Situational Prevention, Criminology, and Social Values." In *Ethical and Social Perspectives on Situational Crime Prevention,* Andrew von Hirsch, David Garland, and Alison Wakefield, eds. Oxford: Hart Publishing.

Clarke, Ronald V. 2001. "Effective Crime Prevention: Keeping Pace with New Developments." *Forum on Crime and Society* 1(1): 17–33.

Clarke, Ronald V. 2007. "Situational Crime Prevention." Paper presented at Home Office conference, Young People and Crime, University of Cambridge, Cambridge, December 12, 2007.

Clarke, Ronald V., and Gisela Bichler-Robertson. 1998. "Place Managers, Slumlords and Crime in Low Rent Apartment Buildings." *Security Journal* 11: 11–19.

Clarke, Ronald V., and Graeme R. Newman. 2006. *Outsmarting the Terrorists.* Westport, Conn.: Praeger Security International.

Clarke, Ronald V., and Ross Homel. 1997. "A Revised Classification of Situational Crime Prevention Techniques." In *Crime Prevention at a Crossroads,* Steven P. Lab, ed. Cincinnati: Anderson.

Clarke, Ronald V., and David Weisburd. 1994. "Diffusion of Crime Control Benefits: Observations on the Reverse of Displacement." In *Crime Prevention Studies,* vol. 2, Ronald V. Clarke, ed. Monsey, N.Y.: Criminal Justice Press.

Clymer, Adam. 2002. "Big Brother vs. Terrorist in Spy Camera Debate." *New York Times,* June 19, 2002. Available at www.nytimes.com.

Cohen, Lawrence E., and Marcus Felson. 1979. "Social Change and Crime Rate Trends: A Routine Activity Approach." *American Sociological Review* 44: 588–608.

Coleman, Roy. 2004. *Reclaiming the Streets: Surveillance, Social Control and the City*. Cullompton, Devon, U.K.: Willan.

Converge Magazine. 2008. "Chicago Links School Cameras to 911 Center." *Converge Magazine*, March 12, 2008. Available at www.convergemag.com.

Cook, Thomas D., and Donald T. Campbell. 1979. *Quasi-Experimentation: Design and Analysis Issues for Field Settings*. Chicago: Rand McNally.

Cornish, Derek B., and Ronald V. Clarke. 1986. "Introduction." In *The Reasoning Criminal: Rational Choice Perspectives on Offending*, Derek B. Cornish and Ronald V. Clarke, eds. New York: Springer-Verlag.

Cornish, Derek B., and Ronald V. Clarke. 2003. "Opportunities, Precipitators and Criminal Decisions: A Reply to Wortley's Critique of Situational Crime Prevention." In *Theory for Practice in Situational Crime Prevention. Crime Prevention Studies*, vol. 16, Martha J. Smith and Derek B. Cornish, eds. Monsey, N.Y.: Criminal Justice Press.

Cozens, Paul M., Richard H. Neale, Jeremy Whitaker, David Hillier, and Max Graham. 2003. "A Critical Review of Street Lighting, Crime and the Fear of Crime in the British City." *Crime Prevention and Community Safety* 5(2): 7–24.

Cramer, Maria. 2008. "Tenants Slam Role of Private Police: Contend Officers Intimidate, Abuse Their Authority." *Boston Globe*, September 1, 2008. Available at www.boston.com.

Cunningham, William C., John J. Strauchs, and Clifford W. Van Meter. 1990. *Private Security Trends, 1970–2000: The Hallcrest Report II*. Boston: Butterworth-Heinemann.

Department of Intergovernmental Fiscal Liaison. 1974. *Final Report—Milwaukee High Intensity Street Lighting Project*. Milwaukee, Wisc.: Department of Intergovernmental Fiscal Liaison.

Ditton, Jason, and Emma Short. 1999. "Yes, it Works, No, it Doesn't: Comparing the Effects of Open-Street CCTV in Two Adjacent Scottish Town Centres." In *Surveillance of Public Space: CCTV, Street Lighting and Crime Prevention. Crime Prevention Studies*, vol. 10, Kate Painter and Nick Tilley, eds. Monsey, N.Y.: Criminal Justice Press.

Donnelly, Patrick G., and Charles E. Kimble. 1997. "Community Organizing, Environmental Change, and Neighborhood Crime." *Crime and Delinquency* 43: 493–511.

Eck, John E. 1995. "A General Model of the Geography of Illicit Retail Marketplaces." In *Crime and Place. Crime Prevention Studies*, vol. 4, John E. Eck and David Weisburd, eds. Monsey, N.Y.: Criminal Justice Press.

Eck, John E. 2006. "Preventing Crime at Places." In *Evidence-Based Crime Prevention*, rev. ed., Lawrence W. Sherman, David P. Farrington, Brandon C. Welsh, and Doris L. MacKenzie, eds. New York: Routledge.

Eck, John E., Ronald V. Clarke, and Rob T. Guerette. 2007. "Risky Facilities: Crime Concentration in Homogeneous Sets of Establishments and Facilities." In *Imagination for Crime Prevention: Essays in Honour of Ken Pease. Crime Prevention Studies*, vol. 21, Graham Farrell, Kate J. Bowers, Shane D. Johnson, and Michael Townsley, eds. Monsey, N.Y.: Criminal Justice Press.

Farrington, David P. 1983. "Randomized Experiments on Crime and Justice." In *Crime and Justice: An Annual Review of Research*, vol. 4, Michael Tonry and Norval Morris, eds. Chicago: University of Chicago Press.

Farrington, David P. 1997. "Evaluating a Community Crime Prevention Program." *Evaluation* 3: 157–173.

Farrington, David P. 2003. "Methodological Quality Standards for Evaluation Research." *Annals of the American Academy of Political and Social Science* 587: 49–68.

Farrington, David P., ed. 2005. *Integrated Developmental and Life-Course Theories of Offending. Advances in Criminological Theory*, vol. 14. New Brunswick, N.J.: Transaction.

Farrington, David P., Trevor H. Bennett, and Brandon C. Welsh. 2007. "The Cambridge Evaluation of the Effects of CCTV on Crime." In *Imagination for Crime Prevention: Essays in Honour of Ken Pease. Crime Prevention Studies*, vol. 21, Graham Farrell, Kate J. Bowers, Shane D. Johnson, and Michael Townsley, eds. Monsey, N.Y.: Criminal Justice Press.

Farrington, David P., Sean Bowen, Abigail Buckle, Tony Burns-Howell, John Burrows, and Martin Speed. 1993. "An Experiment on the Prevention of Shoplifting." In *Crime Prevention Studies*, vol. 1, Ronald V. Clarke, ed. Monsey, N.Y.: Criminal Justice Press.

Farrington, David P., Martin Gill, Sam J. Waples, and Javier Argomaniz. 2007. "The Effects of Closed-Circuit Television on Crime: Meta-Analysis of an English National Quasi-Experimental Multi-Site Evaluation." *Journal of Experimental Criminology* 3: 21–38.

Farrington, David P., Denise C. Gottfredson, Lawrence W. Sherman, and Brandon C. Welsh. 2006. "The Maryland Scientific Methods Scale." In *Evidence-Based Crime Prevention*, rev. ed., Lawrence W. Sherman, David P. Farrington, Brandon C. Welsh, and Doris Layton MacKenzie, eds. New York: Routledge.

Farrington, David P., and Kate Painter. 2003. "How to Evaluate the Impact of CCTV on Crime." *Crime Prevention and Community Safety* 5(3): 7–16.

Farrington, David P., and Anthony Petrosino. 2001. "The Campbell Collaboration Crime and Justice Group." *Annals of the American Academy of Political and Social Science* 578: 35–49.

Farrington, David P., and Brandon C. Welsh. 2002a. *Effects of Improved Street Lighting on Crime: A Systematic Review.* Home Office Research Study, no. 251. London: Home Office.

Farrington, David P., and Brandon C. Welsh. 2002b. "Improved Street Lighting and Crime Prevention." *Justice Quarterly* 19: 313–342.

Farrington, David P., and Brandon C. Welsh. 2004. "Measuring the Effects of Improved Street Lighting on Crime: A Reply to Dr. Marchant." *British Journal of Criminology* 44: 448–467.

Farrington, David P., and Brandon C. Welsh. 2005. "Randomized Experiments in Criminology: What Have We Learned in the Last Two Decades?" *Journal of Experimental Criminology* 1: 9–38.

Farrington, David P., and Brandon C. Welsh. 2006a. "A Half-Century of Randomized Experiments on Crime and Justice." In *Crime and Justice: A Review of Research*, vol. 34, Michael Tonry, ed. Chicago: University of Chicago Press.

Farrington, David P., and Brandon C. Welsh. 2006b. "How Important is 'Regression to the Mean' in Area-Based Crime Prevention Research?" *Crime Prevention and Community Safety* 8(1): 50–60.

Farrington, David P., and Brandon C. Welsh. 2006c. "Improved Street Lighting." In *Preventing Crime: What Works for Children, Offenders, Victims, and Places*, Brandon C. Welsh and David P. Farrington, eds. New York: Springer.

Farrington, David P., and Brandon C. Welsh. 2007. *Saving Children from a Life of Crime: Early Risk Factors and Effective Interventions.* New York: Oxford University Press.

Felson, Marcus, and Ronald V. Clarke. 1997. "The Ethics of Situational Crime Prevention." In *Rational Choice and Situational Crime Prevention: Theoretical Foundations*, Graeme Newman, Ronald V. Clarke, and Shlomo Giora Shoham, eds. Aldershot, U.K.: Ashgate/Dartmouth.

Fleiss, Joseph L. 1981. *Statistical Methods for Rates and Proportions*, 2nd ed. New York: Wiley.

Fleming, Roy, and John N. Burrows. 1986. "The Case for Lighting as a Means of Preventing Crime." *Home Office Research Bulletin* 22: 14–17.

Forst, Brian. 1999. "Policing with Legitimacy, Equity, and Efficiency." In *The Privatization of Policing: Two Views*, Brian Forst and Peter K. Manning. Washington, D.C.: Georgetown University Press.

Fountain, Henry. 2006. "The Camera Never Blinks, but It Multiplies." *New York Times*, April 23, 2006, sect. 4, p. 14.

Gabor, Thomas. 1990. "Crime Displacement and Situational Prevention." *Canadian Journal of Criminology* 32: 41–74.

Garland, David. 2000. "Ideas, Institutions and Situational Crime Prevention." In *Ethical and Social Perspectives on Situational Crime Prevention*, Andrew von Hirsch, David Garland, and Alison Wakefield, eds. Oxford: Hart.

Gest, Ted. 2001. *Crime & Politics: Big Government's Erratic Campaign for Law and Order*. New York: Oxford University Press.

Gill, Martin, and Angela Spriggs. 2005. *Assessing the Impact of CCTV*. Home Office Research Study, no. 292. London: Home Office.

Goldblatt, Peter, and Chris Lewis, eds. 1998. *Reducing Offending: An Assessment of Research Evidence on Ways of Dealing with Offending Behaviour*. Home Office Research Study, no. 187. London: Research and Statistics Directorate, Home Office.

Goldstein, Herman. 1979. "Improving Policing: A Problem-Oriented Approach." *Crime and Delinquency* 25: 236–258.

Goldstein, Herman. 1990. *Problem-Oriented Policing*. Philadelphia: Temple University Press.

Goold, Benjamin J. 2004. *CCTV and Policing: Public Area Surveillance and Police Practices in Britain*. New York: Oxford University Press.

Gottfredson, Denise C., David B. Wilson, and Stacy Skroban Najaka. 2006. "School-Based Crime Prevention." In *Evidence-Based Crime Prevention*, rev. ed., Lawrence W. Sherman, David P. Farrington, Brandon C. Welsh, and Doris Layton MacKenzie, eds. New York: Routledge.

Grandmaison, Rachel, and Pierre Tremblay. 1997. "Évaluation des Effets de la Télé-Surveillance sur la Criminalité Commise dans 13 Stations du Métro de Montréal." *Criminologie* 30: 93–110.

Griffiths, Matthew. n.d. "Town Centre CCTV: An Examination of Crime Reduction in Gillingham, Kent." Unpublished undergraduate dissertation. Reading, U.K.: University of Reading.

Guardian Angels. *Guardian Angels: Beyond the Streets*. 2007. Retrieved January 15, 2008, from www.guardianangels.org/docs/Curtis-brochure.pdf.

Halladay, Mark, and Lisa Bero. 2000. "Implementing Evidence-Based Practice in Health Care." *Public Money and Management* 20: 43–50.

Harcourt, Bernard E. 2001. *Illusion of Order: The False Promise of Broken Windows Policing*. Cambridge, Mass.: Harvard University Press.

Harcourt, Bernard E., and Jens Ludwig. 2006. "Broken Windows: New Evidence from New York City and a Five-City Social Experiment." *University of Chicago Law Review* 73: 271–320.

Harrisburg Police Department. 1976. *Final Evaluation Report of the "High Intensity Street Lighting Program."* Harrisburg, Pa.: Planning and Research

Section, Staff and Technical Services Division, Harrisburg Police Department.

Hauser, Christine. 2008. "Gauging Crime Prevention as Surveillance Expands." *New York Times*, November 4, 2008. Available at http://www.nytimes.com.

Hesseling, René B. P. 1994. "Displacement: A Review of the Empirical Literature." In *Crime Prevention Studies*, vol. 3, Ronald V. Clarke, ed. Monsey, N.Y.: Criminal Justice Press.

Hesseling, René. 1995. "Theft From Cars: Reduced or Displaced?" *European Journal on Criminal Policy and Research* 3(3): 79–92.

Hier, Sean P., Kevin Walby, and Josh Greenberg. 2006. "Supplementing the Panoptic Paradigm: Surveillance, Moral Governance and CCTV." In *Theorizing Surveillance: The Panopticon and Beyond*, David Lyon, ed. Cullompton, Devon, U.K.: Willan.

Home Office Policing and Reducing Crime Unit. 2001. *Invitation to Tender: Evaluation of CCTV Initiatives*. London: Home Office Policing and Reducing Crime Unit.

Hood, John. 2003. "Closed Circuit Television Systems: A Failure in Risk Communication?" *Journal of Risk Research* 6: 233–251.

Hope, Tim. 1995. "Community Crime Prevention." In *Building a Safer Society: Strategic Approaches to Crime Prevention. Crime and Justice: A Review of Research*, vol. 19, Michael Tonry and David P. Farrington, eds. Chicago: University of Chicago Press.

Hough, J. Michael, Ronald V. Clarke, and Patricia Mayhew. 1980. "Introduction." In *Designing Out Crime*, Ronald V. Clarke and Patricia Mayhew, eds. London: Her Majesty's Stationery Office.

Hunter, Ronald D., and C. Ray Jeffrey. 1997. "Preventing Convenience Store Robbery through Environmental Design." In *Situational Crime Prevention: Successful Case Studies*, 2nd ed., Ronald V. Clarke, ed. Guilderland, N.Y.: Harrow and Heston.

Inskeep, Norman R., and Clinton Goff. 1974. *A Preliminary Evaluation of the Portland Lighting Project*. Salem: Oregon Law Enforcement Council.

Jacobs, Jane. 1961. *The Death and Life of Great American Cities*. New York: Random House.

Joh, Elizabeth E. 2004. "The Paradox of Private Policing." *Journal of Criminal Law and Criminology* 95: 49–131.

Johnson, Byron R., Spencer De Li, David B. Larson, and Michael McCullough. 2000. "A Systematic Review of the Religiosity and Delinquency Literature: A Research Note." *Journal of Contemporary Criminal Justice* 16: 32–52.

Jones, Hayley E. 2005. "Measuring Effect Size in Area-Based Crime Prevention Research." Unpublished M.Phil. thesis. Cambridge: Statistical Laboratory, University of Cambridge.

Jones, Trevor, and Tim Newburn. 1998. *Private Security and Public Policing.* Oxford: Clarendon Press.

Kelling, George L., and Catherine M. Coles. 1996. *Fixing Broken Windows: Restoring Order and Reducing Crime in Our Communities.* New York: Simon and Schuster.

Kenney, Dennis Jay. 1986. "Crime on the Subways: Measuring the Effectiveness of the Guardian Angels." *Justice Quarterly* 3: 481–496.

Kinzer, Stephen. 2004. "Chicago Moving to 'Smart' Surveillance Cameras." *New York Times*, September 21, 2004. Available at www.nytimes.com.

Knapp, Martin. 1997. "Economic Evaluations and Interventions for Children and Adolescents with Mental Health Problems." *Journal of Child Psychology and Psychiatry* 38: 3–25.

Koch, Brigitte C. M. 1998. *The Politics of Crime Prevention.* Aldershot, U.K.: Ashgate.

Lasley, James. 1998. *"Designing Out" Gang Homicides and Street Assaults.* Research in Brief, November. Washington, D.C.: National Institute of Justice, U.S. Department of Justice.

Layard, Richard, and Stephen Glaister, eds. 1994. *Cost-Benefit Analysis*, 2nd ed. New York: Cambridge University Press.

Laycock, Gloria, and Claire Austin. 1992. "Crime Prevention in Parking Facilities." *Security Journal* 3(3): 154–160.

Lewis, Edward B., and Tommy T. Sullivan. 1979. "Combating Crime and Citizen Attitudes: A Case Study of the Corresponding Reality. *Journal of Criminal Justice* 7: 71–79.

Lipsey, Mark W., and David B. Wilson. 2001. *Practical Meta-Analysis.* Thousand Oaks, Calif.: Sage.

Lösel, Friedrich, and Peter Koferl. 1989. "Evaluation Research on Correctional Treatment in West Germany: A Meta-Analysis." In *Criminal Behavior and the Justice System: Psychological Perspectives*, Hermann Wegener, Friedrich Lösel, and Jochen Haisch, eds. New York: Springer-Verlag.

MacKenzie, Doris Layton. 2000. "Evidence-Based Corrections: Identifying What Works." *Crime and Delinquency* 46: 457–471.

MacKenzie, Doris Layton. 2006. *What Works in Corrections: Reducing the Criminal Activities of Offenders and Delinquents.* New York: Cambridge University Press.

Manning, Peter K. 1999. "A Dramaturgical Perspective." In *The Privatization of Policing: Two Views*, Brian Forst and Peter K. Manning. Washington, D.C.: Georgetown University Press.

Marchant, P. R. 2004. "A Demonstration that the Claim that Brighter Lighting Reduces Crime is Unfounded." *British Journal of Criminology* 44: 441–447.

Marchant, P. R. 2005. "What Works? A Critical Note on the Evaluation of Crime Reduction Initiatives." *Crime Prevention and Community Safety* 7(2): 7–13.

Marx, Gary T. 1988. *Undercover: Police Surveillance in America*. Berkeley: University of California Press.

Marx, Gary T. 2005. "Camerica? Two Cheers (or Less) for the Indiscriminate Spread of Video Cameras in Public Areas." *ID Trail Mix*, October 2005. Available at idtrail.org.

Mayhew, Patricia, Ronald V. Clarke, John N. Burrows, J. Michael Hough, and Simon W. C. Winchester. 1979. *Crime in Public View*. Home Office Research Study, no. 49. London: Her Majesty's Stationery Office.

Mazerolle, Lorraine, and Janet Ransley. 2005. *Third Party Policing*. New York: Cambridge University Press.

Mazerolle, Lorraine, David C. Hurley, and Mitchell Chamlin. 2002. "Social Behavior in Public Space: An Analysis of Behavioral Adaptations to CCTV." *Security Journal* 15: 59–75.

McCahill, Michael, and Clive Norris. 2002. *CCTV in Britain*. Urbaneye Working Paper, no. 3. Berlin, Germany: Centre for Technology and Society, Technical University Berlin.

McCarthy, Brendan. 2007. "Crime-Fighting Cameras Are the Wrong Focus, Some Say." *Times-Picayune*, March 26, 2007. Available at www.nola.com.

McCord, Joan. 2003. "Cures That Harm: Unanticipated Outcomes of Crime Prevention Programs." *Annals of the American Academy of Political and Social Science* 587: 16–30.

Millenson, Michael L. 1997. *Demanding Medical Excellence: Doctors and Accountability in the Information Age*. Chicago: University of Chicago Press.

Moore, Mark H. 1992. "Problem-solving and Community Policing." In *Modern Policing. Crime and Justice: A Review of Research*, vol. 15, Michael Tonry and Norval Morris, eds. Chicago: University of Chicago Press.

Moore, Mark H. 2002. "The Limits of Social Science in Guiding Policy." *Criminology and Public Policy* 2: 33–42.

Mosteller, Frederick, and Robert F. Boruch, eds. 2002. *Evidence Matters: Randomized Trials in Education Research*. Washington, D.C.: Brookings Institution Press.

Murphy, Dean E. 2002. "As Security Cameras Sprout, Someone's Always Watching." *New York Times*, September 29, 2002, pp. 1, 22.

Musheno, Michael C., James P. Levine, and Denis J. Palumbo. 1978. "Television Surveillance and Crime Prevention: Evaluating an Attempt to Create Defensible Space in Public Housing." *Social Science Quarterly* 58: 647–656.

Newman, Oscar. 1972. *Defensible Space: Crime Prevention through Urban Design.* New York: Macmillan.

Newman, Graeme, Ronald V. Clarke, and Shlomo Giora Shoham, eds. 1997. *Rational Choice and Situational Crime Prevention: Theoretical Foundations.* Aldershot, U.K.: Ashgate/Dartmouth.

Nguyen, Alexander T. 2002. "Here's Looking at You: Has Face-Recognition Technology Completely Outflanked the Fourth Amendment?" *Virginia Journal of Law and Technology* 7: 2–17.

Nieto, Marcus. 1997. *Public Video Surveillance: Is It an Effective Crime Prevention Tool?* Sacramento: California Research Bureau, California State Library.

Nieto, Marcus, Kimberly Johnston-Dodds, and Charlene W. Simmons. 2002. *Public and Private Applications of Video Surveillance and Biometric Technologies.* Sacramento: California Research Bureau, California State Library.

Norris, Clive. 2007. "The Intensification and Bifurcation of Surveillance in British Criminal Justice Policy." *European Journal on Criminal Policy and Research* 13: 139–158.

Norris, Clive, and Gary Armstrong. 1999. *The Maximum Surveillance Society: The Rise of CCTV.* Oxford: Berg.

Norris, Clive, and Michael McCahill. 2006. "CCTV: Beyond Penal Modernism?" *British Journal of Criminology* 46: 97–118.

Painter, Kate. 1994. "The Impact of Street Lighting on Crime, Fear, and Pedestrian Street Use." *Security Journal* 5: 116–124.

Painter, Kate. 1996. "Street Lighting, Crime and Fear of Crime: A Summary of Research." In *Preventing Crime and Disorder: Targeting Strategies and Responsibilities*, Trevor H. Bennett, ed. Cambridge: Institute of Criminology, University of Cambridge.

Painter, Kate, and David P. Farrington. 1997. "The Crime Reducing Effect of Improved Street Lighting: The Dudley Project." In *Situational Crime Prevention: Successful Case Studies*, 2nd ed., Ronald V. Clarke, ed. Guilderland, N.Y.: Harrow and Heston.

Painter, Kate, and David P. Farrington. 1999. "Street Lighting and Crime: Diffusion of Benefits in the Stoke-on-Trent Project." In *Surveillance of Public Space: CCTV, Street Lighting and Crime Prevention. Crime Prevention Studies*, vol. 10, Kate Painter and Nick Tilley, eds. Monsey, N.Y.: Criminal Justice Press.

Painter, Kate, and David P. Farrington. 2001a. "Evaluating Situational Crime Prevention Using a Young People's Survey." *British Journal of Criminology* 41: 266–284.

Painter, Kate, and David P. Farrington. 2001b. "The Financial Benefits of Improved Street Lighting, Based on Crime Reduction." *Lighting Research and Technology* 33: 3–12.

Parenti, Christian. 2003. *The Soft Cage: Surveillance in America from Slavery to the War on Terror.* New York: Basic Books.

Pease, Ken. 1999. "A Review of Street Lighting Evaluations: Crime Reduction Effects." In *Surveillance of Public Space: CCTV, Street Lighting and Crime Prevention. Crime Prevention Studies,* vol. 10, Kate Painter and Nick Tilley, eds. Monsey, N.Y.: Criminal Justice Press.

Pennell, Susan, Christine Curtis, and Joel Henderson. 1986. *Guardian Angels: An Assessment of Citizen Response to Crime.* Washington, D.C.: National Institute of Justice, U.S. Department of Justice.

Pennell, Susan, Christine Curtis, Joel Henderson, and Jeff Tayman. 1989. "Guardian Angels: A Unique Approach to Crime Prevention." *Crime and Delinquency* 35: 378–400.

Petrosino, Anthony. 2000. "How Can We Respond Effectively to Juvenile Crime?" *Pediatrics* 105: 635–637.

Petrosino, Anthony, Robert F. Boruch, Haluk Soydan, Lorna Duggan, and Julio Sanchez-Meca. 2001. "Meeting the Challenges of Evidence-Based Policy: The Campbell Collaboration." *Annals of the American Academy of Political and Social Science* 578: 14–34.

Petrosino, Anthony, Carolyn Turpin-Petrosino, and John Buehler. 2006. "Scared Straight and Other Juvenile Awareness Programs." In *Preventing Crime: What Works for Children, Offenders, Victims, and Places,* Brandon C. Welsh and David P. Farrington, eds. New York: Springer.

Phillips, Coretta. 1999. "A Review of CCTV Evaluations: Crime Reduction Effects and Attitudes towards Its Use." In *Surveillance of Public Space: CCTV, Street Lighting and Crime Prevention. Crime Prevention Studies,* vol. 10, Kate Painter and Nick Tilley, eds. Monsey, N.Y.: Criminal Justice Press.

Piquero, Alex R., David P. Farrington, and Alfred Blumstein. 2003. "The Criminal Career Paradigm." In *Crime and Justice: A Review of Research,* vol. 30, Michael Tonry, ed. Chicago: University of Chicago Press.

Poyner, Barry. 1991. "Situational Crime Prevention in Two Parking Facilities." *Security Journal* 2(2): 96–101.

Poyner, Barry, and Barry Webb. 1997. "Reducing Theft from Shopping Bags in City Center Markets." In *Situational Crime Prevention: Successful Case Studies,* 2nd ed., Ronald V. Clarke, ed. Guilderland, N.Y.: Harrow and Heston.

Quinet, Kenna D., and Samuel Nunn. 1998. "Illuminating Crime: The Impact of Street Lighting on Calls for Police Service." *Evaluation Review* 22: 751–779.

Ramsay, Malcolm, and Rosemary Newton. 1991. *The Effect of Better Street Lighting on Crime and Fear: A Review.* Crime Prevention Unit Paper, no. 29. London: Home Office.

Ratcliffe, Jerry H. 2006. *Video Surveillance of Public Places*. Problem-Oriented Guides for Police Response Guides Series, no. 4. Washington, D.C.: Office of Community Oriented Policing Services, U.S. Department of Justice.

Reppetto, Thomas A. 1976. "Crime Prevention and the Displacement Phenomenon." *Crime and Delinquency* 22: 166–177.

Reuters. 2007. "British Miscreants Caught on Camera Face Loudspeaker Lectures." *New York Times*, April 5, 2007. Available at www.nytimes.com.

Rosen, Jeffrey. 2001. "A Watchful State." *New York Times Magazine*, October 7, 2001. Available at www.nytimes.com.

Rosen, Jeffrey. 2004. *The Naked Crowd: Reclaiming Security and Freedom in an Anxious Age*. New York: Random House.

Rosenbaum, Dennis P., Arthur J. Lurigio, and Robert C. Davis. 1998. *The Prevention of Crime: Social and Situational Strategies*. Belmont, Calif.: Wadsworth.

Safe Neighbourhoods Unit. 1993. *Crime Prevention on Council Estates*. London: Her Majesty's Stationery Office.

Sampson, Robert J., and Janet Lauritsen. 1994. "Violent Victimization and Offending: Individual-, Situational-, and Community-Level Risk Factors." In *Understanding and Preventing Violence. Social Influences*, vol. 3, Albert J. Reiss Jr. and Jeffrey A. Roth, eds. Washington, D.C.: National Academies Press.

Sampson, Robert J., and Stephen W. Raudenbush. 2001. *Disorder in Urban Neighborhoods—Does it Lead to Crime?* Research in Brief, January. Washington, D.C.: National Institute of Justice, U.S. Department of Justice.

Sampson, Robert J., Stephen W. Raudenbush, and Felton Earls. 1997. "Neighborhoods and Violent Crime: A Multilevel Study of Collective Efficacy." *Science* 277: 918–924.

Sarno, Christopher. 1996. "The Impact of Closed Circuit Television on Crime in Sutton Town Centre." In *Towards a Safer Sutton? CCTV One Year On*, Marjorie Bulos and Duncan Grant, eds. London: London Borough of Sutton.

Sarno, Christopher, Michael Hough, and Marjorie Bulos. 1999. *Developing a Picture of CCTV in Southwark Town Centres: Final Report*. London: South Bank University.

Savage, Charlie. 2007. "US Doles Out Millions for Street Cameras: Local Efforts Raise Privacy Concerns." *Boston Globe*, August 12, 2007. Available at www.boston.com.

Schweinhart, Lawrence J., Helen V. Barnes, and David P. Weikart. 1993. *Significant Benefits: The High/Scope Perry Preschool Study through Age 27*. Ypsilanti, Mich.: High/Scope Press.

Shadish, William R., Thomas D. Cook, and Donald T. Campbell. 2002. *Experimental and Quasi-Experimental Designs for Generalized Causal Inference*. Boston: Houghton Mifflin.

Shaftoe, Henry. 1994. "Easton/Ashley, Bristol: Lighting Improvements." In *Housing Safe Communities: An Evaluation of Recent Initiatives*, Steven Osborn, ed. London: Safe Neighbourhoods Unit.

Shearing, Clifford D., and Philip C. Stenning. 1981. "Modern Private Security: Its Growth and Implications." In *Crime and Justice: An Annual Review of Research*, vol. 3, Michael Tonry and Norval Morris, eds. Chicago: University of Chicago Press.

Sherman, Lawrence W. 1995. "Hot Spots of Crime and Criminal Careers of Places." In *Crime and Place. Crime Prevention Studies*, vol. 4, John E. Eck and David Weisburd, eds. Monsey, N.Y.: Criminal Justice Press.

Sherman, Lawrence W. 1998. *Evidence-Based Policing*. Washington, D.C.: Police Foundation.

Sherman, Lawrence W. 2003. "Misleading Evidence and Evidence-Led Policy: Making Social Science More Experimental." *Annals of the American Academy of Political and Social Science* 589: 6–19.

Sherman, Lawrence W., David P. Farrington, Brandon C. Welsh, and Doris L. MacKenzie, eds. 2006. *Evidence-Based Crime Prevention*, rev. ed. New York: Routledge.

Sherman, Lawrence W., Patrick R. Gartin, and Michael E. Buerger. 1989. "Hot Spots of Predatory Crime: Routine Activities and the Criminology of Place." *Criminology* 27: 27–55.

Sherman, Lawrence W., Denise C. Gottfredson, Doris Layton MacKenzie, John E. Eck, Peter Reuter, and Shawn D. Bushway. 1997. *Preventing Crime: What Works, What Doesn't, What's Promising*. Washington, D.C.: National Institute of Justice, U.S. Department of Justice.

Sivarajasingam, Vaseekaran, Jonathan P. Shepherd, and K. Matthews. 2003. "Effect of Urban Closed Circuit Television on Assault Injury and Violence Detection." *Injury Prevention* 9: 312–316.

Skilton, Mike. 1988. *A Better Reception: The Development of Concierge Schemes*. London: Estate Action and Department of the Environment.

Skinns, David. 1998. *Doncaster CCTV Surveillance System: Second Annual Report of the Independent Evaluation*. Doncaster, U.K.: Faculty of Business and Professional Studies, Doncaster College.

Sklansky, David Alan. 1999. "The Private Police." *UCLA Law Review* 46: 1165–1287.

Sklansky, David Alan. 2006. "Private Police and Democracy." *American Criminal Law Review* 43: 89–105.

Sklansky, David Alan. 2008. *Democracy and the Police*. Stanford, Calif.: Stanford University Press.

Skogan, Wesley G. 1990. *Disorder and Decline: Crime and the Spiral of Decay in American Neighborhoods*. New York: Free Press.

Smalley, Suzanne. 2006. "A Force of Their Own: Neighborhood's Private Guards Help Keep the Peace." *Boston Globe*, May 26, 2006. Available at www.boston. com.

Smith, Martha J., Ronald V. Clarke, and Ken Pease. 2002. "Anticipatory Benefits in Crime Prevention." In *Analysis for Crime Prevention. Crime Prevention Studies*, vol. 13, Nick Tilley, ed. Monsey, N.Y.: Criminal Justice Press.

Squires, Peter. 1998. *An Evaluation of the Ilford Town Centre CCTV Scheme*. Brighton, U.K.: Health and Social Policy Research Centre, University of Brighton.

Stanley, Jay, and Barry Steinhardt. 2003. *Bigger Monster, Weaker Chains: The Growth of an American Surveillance Society*. New York: American Civil Liberties Union.

Steele, John. 2005. "With Rucksacks on Their Backs, the Suicide Bombers Go on a Dummy Run." *Telegraph*, September 21, 2005. Available at www.telegraph. co.uk.

Sternhell, Robert. 1977. *The Limits of Lighting: The New Orleans Experiment in Crime Reduction*. Final Impact Evaluation Report. New Orleans, La.: Mayor's Criminal Justice Coordinating Council.

Surette, Ray. 2005. "The Thinking Eye: Pros and Cons of Second Generation CCTV Surveillance Systems." *Policing* 28: 152–173.

Swidey, Neil. 2006. "Private Eyes." *Boston Globe*, April 9, 2006. Available at www. boston.com.

Taub, Richard P., D. Garth Taylor, and Jan D. Dunham. 1984. *Paths of Neighborhood Change: Race and Crime in Urban America*. Chicago: University of Chicago Press.

Taylor, Ralph B. 2006. "Incivilities Reduction Policing, Zero Tolerance, and the Retreat from Coproduction: Weak Foundations and Strong Pressures." In *Police Innovation: Contrasting Perspectives*, David Weisburd and Anthony A. Braga, eds. New York: Cambridge University Press.

Taylor, Ralph B., and Stephen Gottfredson. 1986. "Environmental Design, Crime and Prevention: An Examination of Community Dynamics." In *Communities and Crime. Crime and Justice: A Review of Research*, vol. 8, Albert J. Reiss Jr. and Michael Tonry, eds. Chicago: University of Chicago Press.

Tien, James M., Vincent F. O'Donnell, Arnold Barnett, and Pitu B. Mirchandani. 1979. *Street Lighting Projects: National Evaluation Program*. Phase 1 Report.

Washington, D.C.: National Institute of Law Enforcement and Criminal Justice, U.S. Department of Justice.

Tilley, Nick. 1993. *Understanding Car Parks, Crime and CCTV: Evaluation Lessons from Safer Cities*. Crime Prevention Unit Series Paper, no. 42. London: Home Office.

Tonry, Michael, and David P. Farrington, eds. 1995a. *Building a Safer Society: Strategic Approaches to Crime Prevention. Crime and Justice: A Review of Research*, vol. 19. Chicago: University of Chicago Press.

Tonry, Michael, and David P. Farrington. 1995b. "Strategic Approaches to Crime Prevention." In *Building a Safer Society: Strategic Approaches to Crime Prevention. Crime and Justice: A Review of Research*, vol. 19, Michael Tonry and David P. Farrington, eds. Chicago: University of Chicago Press.

Trasler, Gordon. 1986. "Situational Crime Control and Rational Choice: A Critique." In *Situational Crime Prevention: From Theory into Practice*, Kenneth Heal and Gloria Laycock, eds. London: Her Majesty's Stationery Office.

Trasler, Gordon. 1993. "Conscience, Opportunity, Rational Choice, and Crime." In *Routine Activity and Rational Choice. Advances in Criminological Theory*, vol. 5, Ronald V. Clarke and Marcus Felson, eds. New Brunswick, N.J.: Transaction.

Tremblay, Richard E., and Wendy M. Craig. 1995. "Developmental Crime Prevention." In *Building a Safer Society: Strategic Approaches to Crime Prevention. Crime and Justice: A Review of Research*, vol. 19, Michael Tonry and David P. Farrington, eds. Chicago: University of Chicago Press.

U.S. General Accountability Office. 2003. *Youth Illicit Drug Use Prevention: DARE Long-Term Evaluations and Federal Efforts to Identify Effective Programs*. Report GAO-03–172R. Washington, D.C.: U.S. General Accountability Office.

van Andel, Henk. 1989. "Crime Prevention That Works: The Care of Public Transport in the Netherlands." *British Journal of Criminology* 29: 47–56.

van Dijk, Jan, J. M. 1995. "Police, Private Security and Employee Surveillance: Trends and Prospects, with Special Emphasis on the Case of the Netherlands." In *Changes in Society, Crime and Criminal Justice in Europe: A Challenge for Criminological Education and Research. Crime and Insecurity in the City*, vol. 1, Cyrille Fijnaut, Johan Goethals, Tony Peters, and Lode Walgrave, eds. The Hague, Netherlands: Kluwer.

von Hirsch, Andrew. 2000. "The Ethics of Public Television Surveillance." In *Ethical and Social Perspectives on Situational Crime Prevention*, Andrew von Hirsch, David Garland, and Alison Wakefield, eds. Oxford: Hart.

Vrij, Albert, and Frans W. Winkel. 1991. "Characteristics of the Built Environment and Fear of Crime: A Research Note on Interventions in Unsafe Locations." *Deviant Behavior* 12: 203–215.

Wagner, Allen E. 1997. "A Study of Traffic Pattern Modifications in an Urban Crime Prevention Program." *Journal of Criminal Justice* 25: 19–30.

Wakefield, Alison. 2003. *Selling Security: The Private Policing of Public Space.* Cullompton, Devon, U.K.: Willan.

Waples, Sam, and Martin Gill. 2006. "The Effectiveness of Redeployable CCTV." *Crime Prevention and Community Safety* 8(1): 1–16.

Washington Post. 2007. "Surveillance Cameras: Fighting Crime or Invading Privacy?" ABC News-*Washington Post* Poll. Available at media. washingtonpost.com/wp-srv/politics/ssi/polls/postpoll_072307.html.

Webb, Barry, and Gloria Laycock. 1992. *Reducing Crime on the London Underground: An Evaluation of Three Pilot Projects.* Crime Prevention Unit Series Paper, no. 30. London: Home Office.

Weimer, David L., and Lee S. Friedman. 1979. "Efficiency Considerations in Criminal Rehabilitation Research: Costs and Consequences." In *The Rehabilitation of Criminal Offenders: Problems and Prospects*, Lee Sechrest, Susan O. White, and Elizabeth D. Brown, eds. Washington, D.C.: National Academy of Sciences.

Weinrott, Mark R., Richard R. Jones, and James R. Howard. 1982. "Cost-Effectiveness of Teaching Family Programs for Delinquents: Results of a National Evaluation." *Evaluation Review* 6: 173–201.

Weisburd, David. 2005. "Hot Spots Policing Experiments and Criminal Justice Research: Lessons from the Field." *Annals of the American Academy of Political and Social Science* 599: 220–245.

Weisburd, David, Cynthia M. Lum, and Anthony Petrosino. 2001. "Does Research Design Affect Study Outcomes in Criminal Justice?" *Annals of the American Academy of Political and Social Science* 578: 50–70.

Weisburd, David, Laura A. Wyckoff, Justin Ready, John E. Eck, Joshua C. Hinkle, and Frank Gajewski. 2006. "Does Crime Just Move around the Corner? A Controlled Study of Spatial Displacement and Diffusion of Crime Control Benefits." *Criminology* 44: 549–592.

Welsh, Brandon C., and David P. Farrington. 2000. "Monetary Costs and Benefits of Crime Prevention Programs." In *Crime and Justice: A Review of Research*, vol. 27, Michael Tonry, ed. Chicago: University of Chicago Press.

Welsh, Brandon C., and David P. Farrington. 2001. "Toward an Evidence-Based Approach to Preventing Crime." *Annals of the American Academy of Political and Social Science* 578: 158–173.

Welsh, Brandon C., and David P. Farrington. 2002. *Crime Prevention Effects of Closed Circuit Television: A Systematic Review.* Home Office Research Study, no. 252. London: Home Office.

Welsh, Brandon C., and David P. Farrington. 2003. "Effects of Closed-Circuit Television on Crime." *Annals of the American Academy of Political and Social Science* 587: 110–135.

Welsh, Brandon C., and David P. Farrington. 2004a. "Evidence-Based Crime Prevention: The Effectiveness of CCTV." *Crime Prevention and Community Safety* 6(1): 21–33.

Welsh, Brandon C., and David P. Farrington. 2004b. "Surveillance for Crime Prevention in Public Space: Results and Policy Choices in Britain and America." *Criminology and Public Policy* 3: 497–526.

Welsh, Brandon C., and David P. Farrington. 2006a. "Evidence-Based Crime Prevention." In *Preventing Crime: What Works for Children, Offenders, Victims, and Places*, Brandon C. Welsh and David P. Farrington, eds. New York: Springer.

Welsh, Brandon C., and David P. Farrington. 2006b. "Closed-Circuit Television Surveillance." In *Preventing Crime: What Works for Children, Offenders, Victims, and Places*, Brandon C. Welsh and David P. Farrington, eds. New York: Springer.

Welsh, Brandon C., and David P. Farrington, eds. 2006c. *Preventing Crime: What Works for Children, Offenders, Victims, and Places*. New York: Springer.

Welsh, Brandon C., David P. Farrington, and Lawrence W. Sherman, eds. 2001. *Costs and Benefits of Preventing Crime*. Boulder, Colo.: Westview Press.

Wikström, Per-Olof H. 1998. "Communities and Crime." In *The Handbook of Crime and Punishment*, Michael Tonry, ed. New York: Oxford University Press.

Williamson, Douglas, and Sara McLafferty. 2000. "The Effects of CCTV on Crime in Public Housing: An Application of GIS and Spatial Statistics." Paper presented at the annual meeting of the American Society of Criminology, San Francisco, November 2000.

Williams, Katherine S., and Craig Johnstone. 2000. "The Politics of the Selective Gaze: Closed Circuit Television and the Policing of Public Space." *Crime, Law and Social Change* 34: 183–200.

Wilson, David B. 2001. "Meta-Analytic Methods for Criminology." *Annals of the American Academy of Political and Social Science* 578: 71–89.

Wilson, Dean, and Adam Sutton. 2003. *Open-Street CCTV in Australia*. Trends and Issues in Crime and Criminal Justice, no. 271. Canberra: Australian Institute of Criminology.

Wilson, James Q., and George L. Kelling. 1982. "Broken Windows: The Police and Neighborhood Safety." *Atlantic Monthly*, March 1982, pp. 29–38.

Winge, Stig, and Johannes Knutsson. 2003. "An Evaluation of the CCTV Scheme at Oslo Central Railway Station." *Crime Prevention and Community Safety* 5(3): 49–59.

Winton, Richard. 2006. "LAPD Adds 10 Cameras to Curb Skid Row Crime: Expanded System Will Make Downtown the Most Highly Monitored Part of the City." *Los Angeles Times*, September 15, 2006. Available at www.latimes.com.

Wolfe, Elizabeth. 2002. "Sniper Eludes Police Despite Video." *Washington Post*, October 17, 2002. Available at www.washingtonpost.com.

Wright, Roger, Martin Heilweil, Paula Pelletier, and Karen Dickinson. 1974. *The Impact of Street Lighting on Crime*. Ann Arbor: University of Michigan.

Zahm, Diane L. 2004. "Brighter Is Better. Or Is It? The Devil Is in the Details." *Criminology and Public Policy* 3: 535–546.

Index